Easy Crafts for Home & Family 2

SALLYMILNER
PUBLISHING

First published in 2003 by
Sally Milner Publishing Pty Ltd
PO Box 2104
Bowral NSW 2576
AUSTRALIA

© Sally Milner Publishing Pty Ltd, 2003

Design by Anna Warren, Warren Ventures Pty Ltd
Illustrations by Wendy Gorton and Anna Warren
Printed in China

National Library of Australia Cataloguing-in-Publication data:

Easy crafts for home & family 2.

   ISBN 1 86351 310 8.

   1. Handicraft. (Series : Milner craft series).

  745.5

10 9 8 7 6 5 4 3 2 1

CONTENTS

For the baby

Easy for the children

Soft furnishings

In the sewing basket

Embroidery

Christmas is for giving

Knitting

Home decorating

General crafts

Quilting

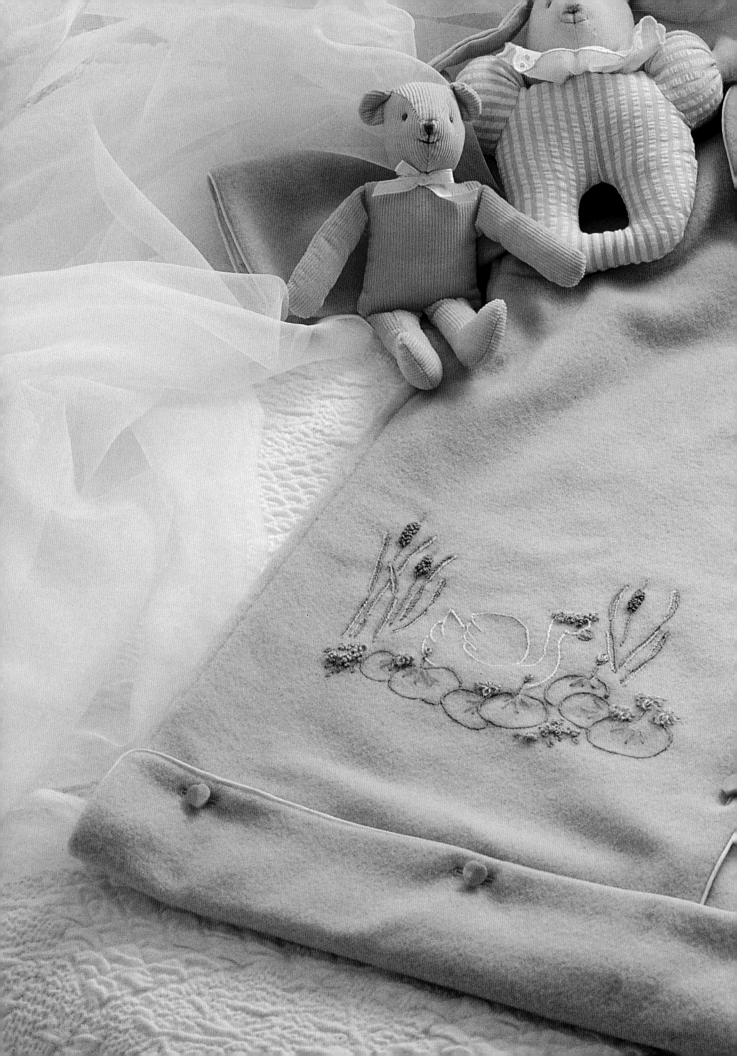

FOR THE BABY

Baby Bears

A beautiful baby bear for that special baby.

MATERIALS

23 cm (¼ yard) of 115 cm (45 in) wide cotton

Synthetic stuffing

Scraps of felt for eyes

Embroidery floss

Paper or thin cardboard for pattern

Note: Seam 1 cm (⅜ in) deep with right sides together. Clip seam allowance at curves.

DIRECTIONS

1 Pattern: Enlarge pattern pieces to actual size and add 1 cm (⅜ in) seam allowances all around. Cut out a pair (2) or 2 pairs (4) from folded fabric.

2 Sew each pair of arm and leg pieces together, leaving upper straight edge open. Turn and stuff firmly.

3 Sew each pair of body sections together along one curved edge. Sew two halves of body together leaving neck edge open. Turn and stuff firmly.

4 Sew ear pieces together around curved edge. Turn and stuff lightly. Sew centre front and back head seams. Join front and back head. Turn and stuff firmly.

5 Using doubled thread, gather neck edge of body. Pull up and secure.

6 Pin arms, legs, head and ears to body turning under the raw edges. Slipstitch securely.

7 Fasten round felt eyes to head with buttonhole stitch. Embroider nose in satin stitch, and mouth in chain or stem stitch.

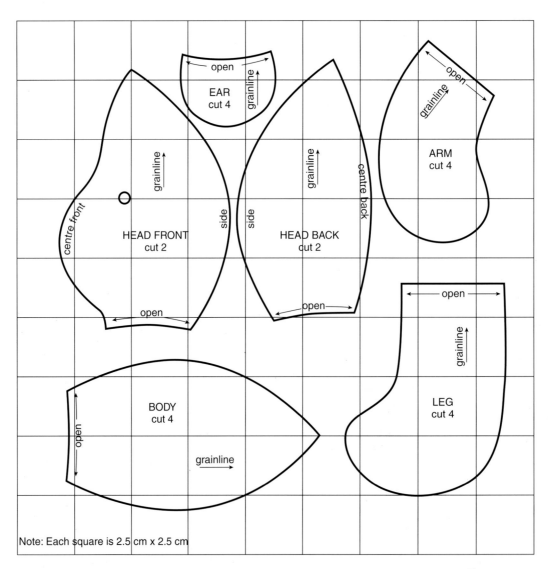

Note: Each square is 2.5 cm x 2.5 cm

Baby Bunny

Make a whole family of these cute bunnies.

MATERIALS

Scrap of cotton fabric
Polyester fibrefill for stuffing
20 cm (8 in) of 1.3 cm (½ in) wide ribbon
Embroidery floss
Tracing paper

DIRECTIONS

1 Trace full-size pattern onto tracing paper.

2 From fabric, cut out two bunny shapes, 1 cm (⅜ in) seam allowed. Embroider face on bunny, using satin stitch for eyes and nose, and stem stitch for mouth.

3 Sew front and back together, with right sides facing and leaving a small opening for turning below arm. Reinforce corners with second row of stitching. Clip seams, turn and press.

4 Stuff lightly with fibrefill. Slipstitch opening closed. Tie bow around neck.

Baby's Overalls

Your special little person will look fabulous in these easy-to-make overalls.

To fit baby aged 6 to 12 months

MATERIALS

90 cm (1 yd) of 115 cm (45 in) wide cotton fabric

12.5 cm x 30 cm (5 in x 12 in) iron-on interfacing

4.1 m (4 ½ yd) of 3 mm (⅛ in) wide piping cord

Two 1.3 cm (½ in) wide buttons

30 cm (12 in) of 1.5 cm (⅝ in) wide elastic

Tracing paper and pencil

Note: To 'cut a pair', pin the pattern to folded fabric. Seam 1 cm (⅜ in) deep with pieces pinned right sides together.

DIRECTIONS

1 *Cutting*: Copy the patterns on page 13 and make to size using scale. With its CF line on a fold of fabric, cut two bibs. Cut one pair each of pants and leg facings (using pants pattern).

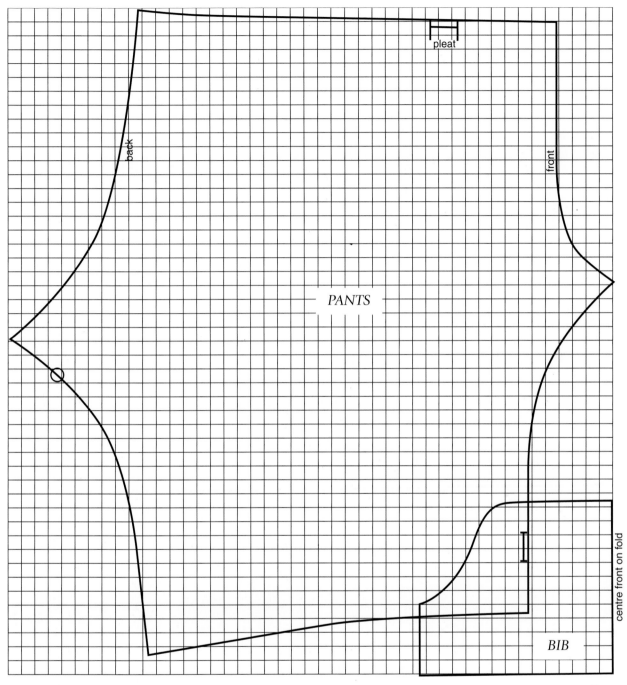

pleat

back

front

PANTS

centre front on fold

BIB

Cut two each of straps and strap facings, each 5 cm x 50 cm (2 in x 20 in). Cut a 7.5 cm x 30 cm (3 in x 12 in) back casing and a 10 cm x 15.5 cm (4 in x 6 in) pocket and about 4.1 m (4 ½ yd) (pieced on the straight grain) of 3.8 cm (1 ½ in) wide bias strip to cover piping cord.

2 *Preparations:* Iron interfacing to wrong side of a bib piece; trim edges flush. Fold the bias strip over the cord, right side out and raw edges even, and stitch with a zipper foot through both layers against the cord.

3 *Pocket:* With right sides together, turn over 5 cm (2 in)

Note: Each square is 1 cm x 1 cm

13

to make a square; seam down both short ends. Turn it right side out, turn under raw edges, press and edgestitch pocket to one overall piece (see pattern).

4 *Pants*: Seam pants together at the back crotch, then front crotch edges. Fold the piece so the seams are matched and centred, then stitch the inner leg seams. With raw edges even, baste piping over the bottom edge of each pant leg. Seam short ends of each leg facing and pin it over the piping, with seams matching; stitch. Turn facings inside, hem them and turn up the cuffs. At the waist, fold and baste the pleats (see pattern). Stitch piping to pants, raw edges even.

5 *Bib*: Baste piping over the curved, top edges of the bib, raw edges even. Stitch facing on top, right sides together. Turn and press; topstitch in the piping seam.

6 *Casing*: With lower edges even and right sides together, stitch one end of the casing to each side edge of the bib. Stitch them to the pants, matching CF's. Turn up the raw edge of casing 6 mm (¼ in), fold it down just beyond the waist seam and stitch. Thread elastic through the casing and stitch twice across each end, adjusting its length to fit. Press raw edges toward bib; turn under raw edge of bib facing and slipstitch.

7 *Straps*: Pipe and face the straps, leaving one end open. Turn, press and topstitch. Crossing the straps diagonally, pin each open end to the back casing; stitch securely. Make two buttonholes (see pattern) and sew a button to each strap.

Baby's Shoes

Size 6 to 12 months

MATERIALS

20 cm x 50 cm (8 in x 20 in) each of outer fabric and lining

20 cm x 50 cm (8 in x 20 in) of iron-on interfacing

2 buttons 1.3 cm (½ in) or smaller

Tracing paper

Note: With right sides facing, seam 6 mm (¼ in) from the raw edges. Clip the seam allowance at curves.

DIRECTIONS

1 *Cutting*: Trace the two full-size patterns shown. Placing its centre back on a fold of fabric, cut two uppers each from the outer fabric, lining and interfacing. Cut two soles from the same three fabrics.

2 *Interfacing*: Iron the interfacing to the wrong side of the outer pieces.

3 *Seaming*: Sew the centre front seam (A to B) of each upper. Press it open. Turn it right side out and topstitch at each side of the seam. Seam a sole to each upper, matching centres at B and C. Press open.

4 *Lining*: Repeat Step 3 with lining pieces. With right sides together, pin the lining over the shoe, matched at CB and CF and edges even. Stitch the raw edges, seams, turn and edgestitch.

5 *Buttons*: Make buttonholes and sew on the buttons.

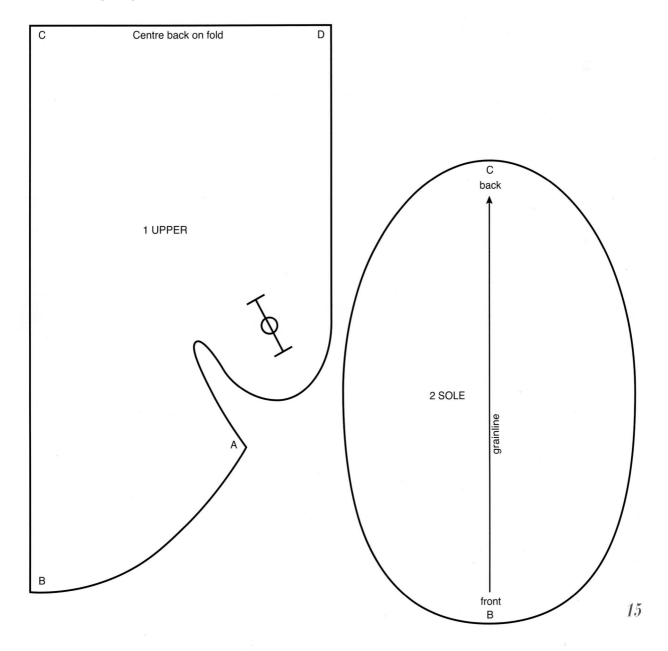

Baby's Sleeping Bag

This sleeping bag is a wonderful way to keep your little one warm through the first winter.

Fits size: 3 to 6 months

MATERIALS

1 m (40 in) of gown blanketing

1.7 m (68 in) of matching Swiss Nelona

4.1 m (4½ yd) of piping cord

Appleton's Crewel Wool: White, Lemon, Pale Blue, Pale Green, Green, Light Brown, Yellow

Pink Gossamer mohair

Piecemakers tapestry needle

Transfer pencil

Eight buttons

Sewing thread to match the fabric

Tracing paper

Pencil

METHOD

See the pattern and the embroidery design on pages 17–21.

PREPARATION

1 Trace the pattern pieces. Cut out the pattern pieces from the gown blanketing.

2 Transfer the main embroidery design onto one of the fronts so the design sits 14 cm (5 ½ in) from the bottom edge. You will need to reverse the design for the other front.

Note: Take care when transferring the design that the iron is not too hot or you might scorch the fabric.

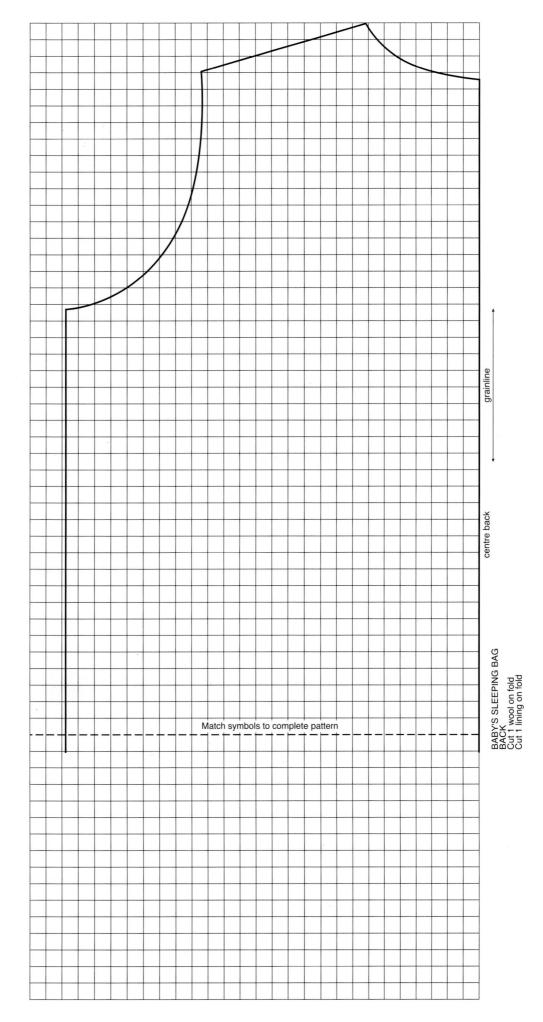

grainline

centre back

Match symbols to complete pattern

BABY'S SLEEPING BAG
BACK
Cut 1 wool on fold
Cut 1 lining on fold

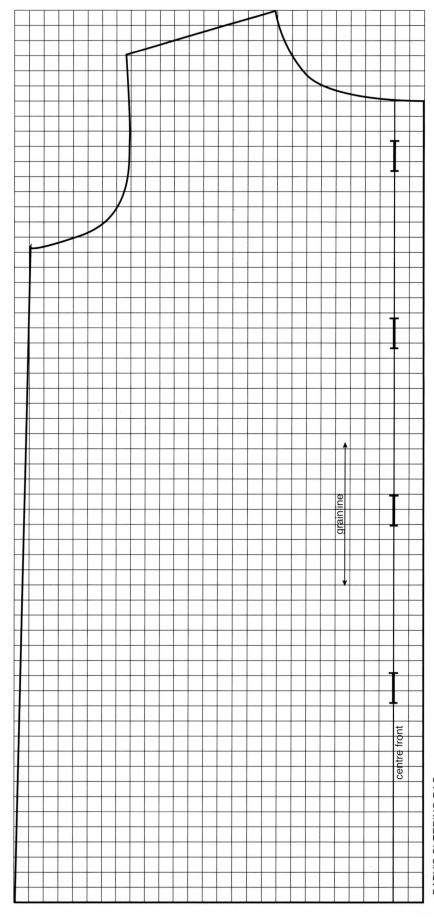

BABY'S SLEEPING BAG
FRONT
Cut 2 wool
Cut 2 lining

grainline

centre front

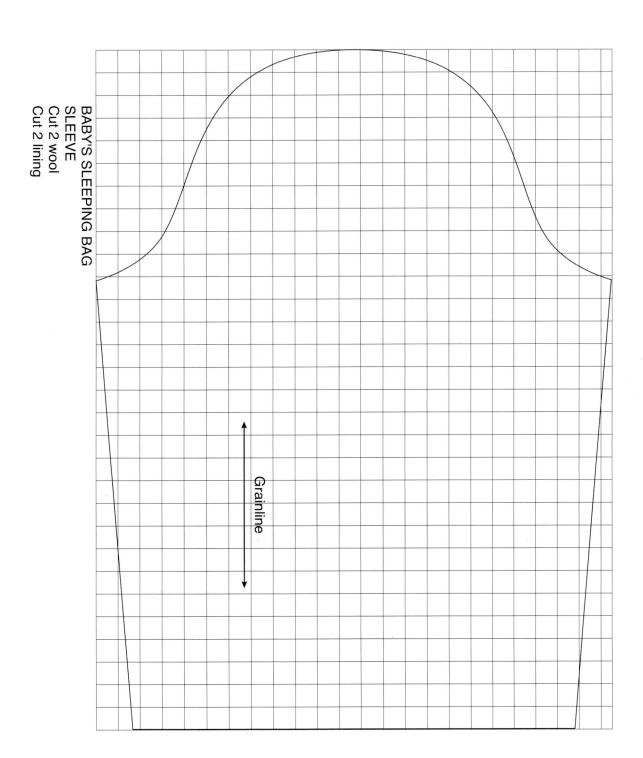

BABY'S SLEEPING BAG
SLEEVE
Cut 2 wool
Cut 2 lining

Grainline

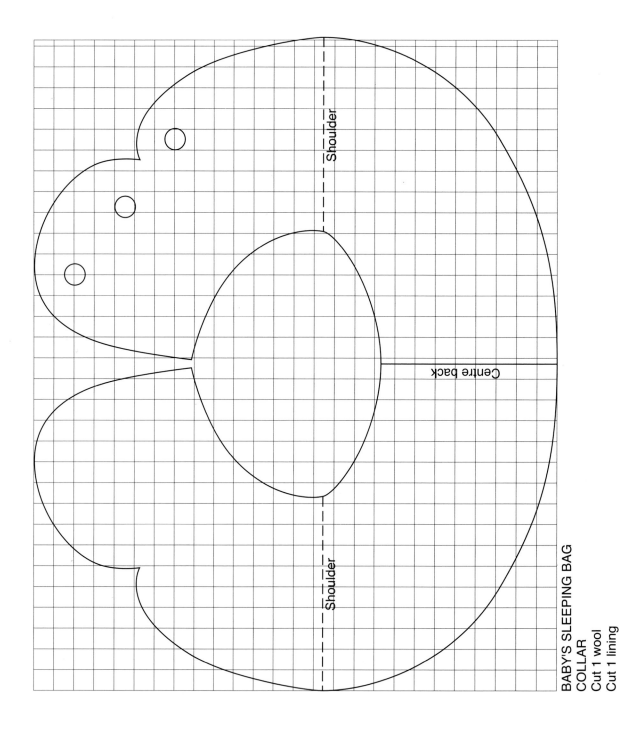

Shoulder

Centre back

Shoulder

BABY'S SLEEPING BAG
COLLAR
Cut 1 wool
Cut 1 lining

EMBROIDERY

1 Stitch the swans and stems in stem stitch. Stitch the leaves in stem stitch, using Pale Green on one side and Green on the other.

2 Stitch the reeds and garlands in French knots.

3 Stitch the waterlilies in lazy daisy stitch placing two petals

on each side and a fifth petal in the centre, overlapping the others (Fig. 1). For the centre of the waterlily, work three pistil stitches in Lemon.

4 Embroider the garlands on the collar piece, surrounded by leaves in detached chain stitches (Fig. 2). Stitch the forget-me-nots in Pale Blue French knots with Lemon French knot centres.

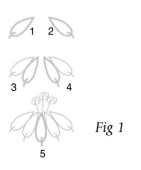

Fig 1

Fig 2

SEWING

1 Using the pattern, cut out the lining pieces from the Nelona. From the remaining Nelona, cut 3 cm (1 ⅛ in) wide bias strips. Join them together then cover the piping cord with the joined bias.

2 Pin the piping to the right side of the collar around the scallops, 1 cm (⅜ in) from the edge. Clip into the seam allowance of the piping to allow it to curve gently but take care not to clip the stitching. Stitch the piping into place.

3 Place the collar and the collar lining together with the right sides facing. Sew them together around the scalloped edge, stitching in the stitching line of the piping. Clip both the collar and the lining, then turn the collar right side out. Press gently on the wrong side.

4 Join the fronts and back at the shoulders. Sew in the sleeves, then join the side seams. Make the lining in the same way.

5 Stitch the piping around the right side of the sleeve ends and around the front opening and the flap. Sew the collar to the neck edge, using a 1 cm (³⁄₈ in) seam.

6 Place the outer piece and the lining together with the right sides facing. Stitch them together around the sleeve ends, as close as possible to the piping stitching line, and around the front opening and flap edges. Do not stitch across the neck edge.

7 Turn the sleeping bag right side out through the neck opening. Fold over the seam allowance at the neck edge of the lining, clipping where necessary. Slipstitch the lining to the neck edge.

8 Make eight buttonholes and sew on the buttons to correspond.

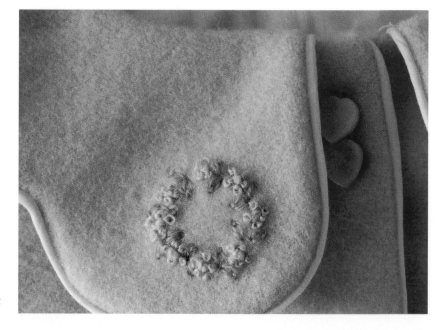

Booties with Ribbed Ankle

Little feet will keep cosy warm through those first few months with these gorgeous booties.

Technique: knitting

Size: Directions given are for size 0 to 6 months.

Note: For slightly smaller booties use one size smaller needles and for slightly larger booties use one size larger needles than suggested to obtain the correct gauge.

MATERIALS
Fingering-Weight Yarn (50 gr ball): 1 ball each of main colour (Mc) and contrasting colour (A); 1 pair of No. 3 knitting needles, or any size needles to obtain gauge below: 90 cm (1 yd) of 6 mm (¼ in) wide ribbon; tapestry needle.

GAUGE
On No. 3 needles in stockinette stitch (st st) 8 sts = 2.54 cm (1 in); 11 rows = 2.54 cm (1 in). Be sure to check your gauge.

DIRECTIONS
Using No. 3 needles and Mc, cast on 43 sts.

Row 1: (K1, inc in next st, k 18 inc in next st) twice, k 1–47 sts.

Row 2 and all even numbered rows: knit

Row 3: (K 1, inc in next st, k 20, inc in next st) twice, k 1.

Row 5: (K 1, inc in next st, k 22, inc in next st) twice, k 1.

Row 7: (K 1, inc in next st, k 24, inc in next st) twice, k 1.

Row 9: (K 1, inc in next st, k 26, inc in next st) twice, k 1.

Row 11: (K 1, inc in next st, k 28, inc in next st) twice, k 1.

Row 12: K 2 tog, k 63, k 2 tog—65sts.

Work 10 rows st st (k 1 row, p 1 row)

Instep shaping:

Next row: K 37, k 2 tog, turn.

Next row: Sl 1, p 9, p 2 tog, turn.

Next row: Sl 1, k 9, k 2 tog, turn.

Repeat last two rows until 45 sts rem (17 sts on each side of instep).

Next row: Sl 1, k 9, k 2 tog, k 16.

Next row: Purl—44 sts.

Ankle:

Next row: K 1, *yo, k 2 tog, rep from * to last st, k 1.

Next row: Using A, purl, inc one st at each end—46 sts.

Next row: K 2, *p 2, k 2, rep from * to end.

Next row: P 2, *k 2, p2, rep from * to end.

Rep last 2 rows until rib section measures 8 cm (3 ¼ in) from beg, working last row on wrong side.

Bind off.

FINISHING
Sew foot and back seam, reversing back seam for 3.8 cm (1 ½ in) at ankle length. Thread ribbon through eyelet holes and tie in a bow. Fold rib section in half onto right side.

Fair Isle

Fair Isle is a small island off the coast of Scotland, which has given its name to a very easily recognizable coloured knitting pattern. Local legend has it that the colours and intricate patterns were based on those worn by Spanish sailors shipwrecked on the island after the defeat of the Spanish Armada in 1588. Others hold that the patterns were handed down by Viking explorers from Scandinavia.

A true Fair Isle pattern usually has two colours to a row and uses a Shetland wool called 'fingering'. In the past the lovely colours of Fair Isle were dyed with natural dyes. These days chemical dyes are used to reproduce traditional colours. Classic Fair Isle patterns have been repeated unchanged for generations.

Fair Isle Crib Blanket

Size: 62.5 cm x 97.5 cm (25 in x 39 in)

MATERIALS
Sport-weight yarn (50 gr ball):
9 balls of white (Mc), 3 balls of blue (A), 1 ball each of apricot (B), lilac (C) and coral (D); 1 pair each No. 5 and No. 6 knitting needles, or any size needles to obtain gauge below; length of batting about 61 cm x 97.5 cm (24 in x 39 in), tapestry needle.

GAUGE
On No. 5 needles in stockinette stitch (st st)—
13 sts = 5 cm (2 in),
9 rows = 2.54 cm (1 in).
On No. 6 needles in pattern stitch—13 sts = 5 cm (2 in),
9 rows = 2.54 cm (1 in).
Be sure to check your gauge.

Note: When changing colours, pick up new colour from under the colour being used, twisting yarns on wrong side of work to

prevent holes. Carry colour not in use loosely across wrong side of work to end of row, being careful to maintain gauge.

DIRECTIONS

Using No. 6 needles and Mc, cast on 161 sts.

Beg Fair Isle Pattern:

Row 1: K 4 Mc, *k 3 A, k 3 Mc; rep from * to last st, k 1 Mc.

Row 2: P 4 Mc *p 3 A, p 3 Mc; rep from * to last st, k 1 Mc.

Rows 3 and 4: Rep Rows 1 and 2 once.

Rows 5- 8: Rep Rows 1 and 2 twice, using A in place of Mc, and Mc in place of A.

Rep Rows 1 to 8 once.

Row 17: K 4 Mc, k 3 A, k 3 Mc, k 3 A, k 3 B, *k 3 Mc, k 3 B; rep from * to last 13 sts, k 3 A, k 3 Mc k 3 A, k 4 Mc.

Row 18: P 4 Mc, p 3 A, p 3 Mc, p 3 A, p 3 B, *p 3 Mc, p 3 B; rep from * to last 13 sts, p 3 A, p 3 Mc, p 3 A, p 4 Mc.

Rows 19 and 20: Rep last 2 rows once.

Row 21: K 4 A, k 3 Mc, k 3 A, k 3 Mc, k 3 B. *k 3 Mc, k 3 B; rep from * to last 13 sts, k 3, Mc, k 3 A, k 3 Mc, k 4 A.

Row 22: P 4 A, p 3 Mc, p 3 A, p 3 Mc, p 3 B, *p 3 Mc, p 3 B; rep from * to last 13 sts, p 3 Mc, p 3 A, p 3 Mc, p 4 A.

Rows 23 and 24: Rep last 2 rows once.

Row 25: K 4 Mc, k 3 A, k 3 Mc, k 3 A, *k 8 C, k 1 Mc; rep from * to last 13 sts, k 3 A, k 3 Mc, k 3 A, k 4 Mc.

Row 26: P 4 Mc, p 3 A, p 3 Mc, p 3 A, *p 2 Mc, p 7 C; rep from * to last 13 sts, p 3 A, p 3 Mc, p 3 A, p 4 Mc.

Row 27: K 4 Mc, k 3 A, k 3 Mc, k 3 A, *k 6 C, k 3 Mc; rep from * to last 13 sts, k 3 A, k 3 Mc, k 3 A, k 4 Mc.

Row 28: P 4 Mc, p 3 A, p 3 Mc, p 3 A, *p 4 Mc, p 5 C; rep from * to last 13 sts, p 3 A, p 3 Mc, p 3 A, p 4 Mc.

Row 29: K 4 A, k 3 Mc, k 3 A, k 3 Mc, *k 4 C, k 5 C; rep from * to last 13 sts, k 3 Mc, k 3 A, k 3 Mc, k 4 A.

Row 30: P 4 A, p 3 Mc, p 3 A, p 3 Mc, *p 6 Mc, p 3 C; rep from * to last 13 sts, p 3 Mc, p 3 A, p 3 Mc, p 4 A.

Row 31: K 4 A, k 3 Mc, k 3 A, k 3 Mc, *k 2 C, k 7 Mc; rep from * to last 13 sts, k 3 Mc, k 3 A, k 3 Mc, k 4 A.

Row 32: P 4 A, p 3 Mc, p 3 A, p 3 Mc, *p 8 Mc, p 1 C; rep from * to last 13 sts, p 3 Mc, p 3 A, p 3 Mc, p 4 A.

Rep Rows 1– 8 twice.

Rep Rows 25 to 32 once, keeping colours as established in border pat, but use D in place of Mc, and Mc in place of C for triangle pattern.

Rep Rows 17 to 24 once.

Last 64 rows form pattern stitch.

Continue in pat until work measures about 97.5 cm (39 in) from beg, ending with Row 8 or Row 40.

Using Mc, work in st (k 1 row, p 1 row) until Mc section measures same as Fair Isle pattern section, ending with a purl row.

Bind off loosely.

FINISHING

Fold knitting in half (foldline is at end of Fair Isle pat section), so that right sides are together. Sew 2 sides together and turn inside out. Place batting inside and slipstitch rem side closed. Using 2 strands of A and small even running stitches, sew around inside of border, through all 3 thicknesses (including batting).

Giant Pink Bunny

The giant pink bunny is about 46 cm (18 in) when seated.

MATERIALS

2.5 m (2 yd 28 in) of 115 cm (45 in) wide cotton fabric

Synthetic stuffing

Embroidery floss

Black and white felt scraps

Tracing paper

Sewing thread

Note: Seam 1 cm (³⁄₈ in) deep with pieces pinned right sides together.

DIRECTIONS

1 *Cutting*: Trace and enlarge patterns, Nos 1 through 9, including labels. Cut 1 pair each of #1 body front, #3 upper back, #4 side head and #9 upper leg. Cut two #8 soles. Cut one each of #5 head gusset and #2 back lower body and legs and four each of #6 ears and #7 arms.

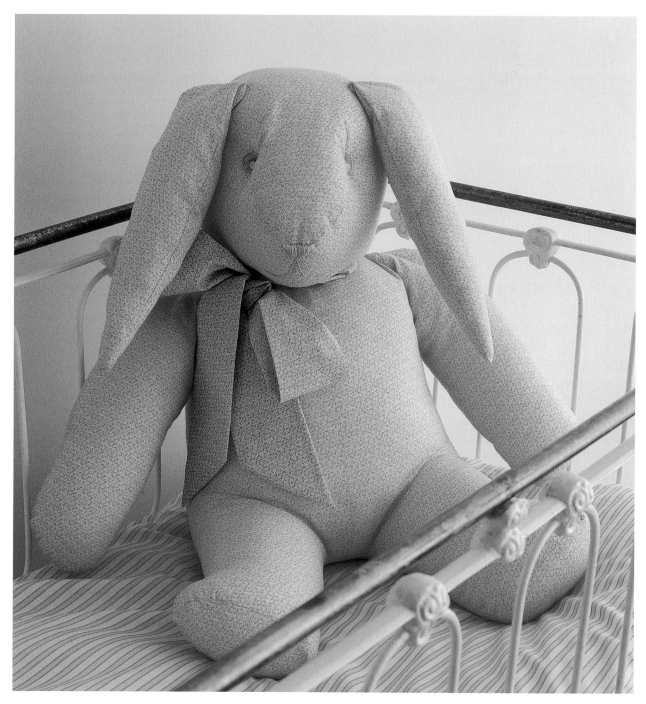

2 *Head*: Stitch the head darts, press them open. Seam side heads from nose down to the larger dart. Matching 'noses', seam the gusset between them, leaving a 5 cm (2 in) back opening. Turn right side out, stuff it and slipstitch it closed.

3 *Back and Front*: With a CB (centre back) edge at each dart edge, seam the short edge of each upper back to the lower back. Stitch the dart and continue up the CB seam, stopping 5 cm (2 in) down from the top point. Seam front bodies at CF (centre front) edge. With the foot facing outward, baste top of each upper leg to lower edge of front body; stitch.

4 *Arms*: Seam the straight edge of an arm to each side of the body front, starting 2.54 cm (1 in) down from the top point. Repeat, to match, at back body.

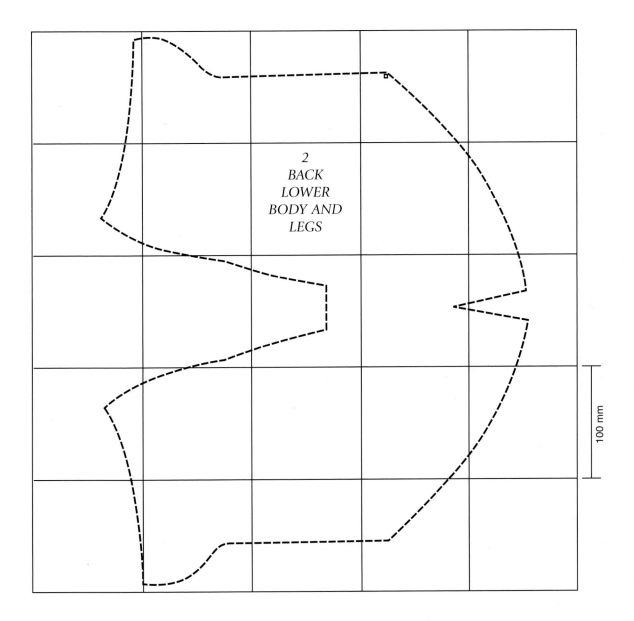

2
BACK
LOWER
BODY AND
LEGS

100 mm

5 *Body*: Pin front body to back body except at foot bottoms. Clip to crotch corners. Seam a sole to each foot. Turn right side out and stuff. Slipstitch opening closed.

6 *Head*: Pin head on body and, in a kind of oval, sew it by hand along the pins. Seam each pair of ears together except at the short edge. Turn under the raw edge and sew it by hand over a head dart, opening the edge to a shallow oval.

7 *Face*: Embroider a satin-stitch nose and a chain-stitch mouth (see photo). Contour eye sockets by stitching from one eye to the other with strong thread, pulling it up slightly before you fasten the end. Slipstitch a 6 mm (¼ in) black circle to a 1.3 cm (½ in) white circle, then slipstitch that to the head. Repeat.

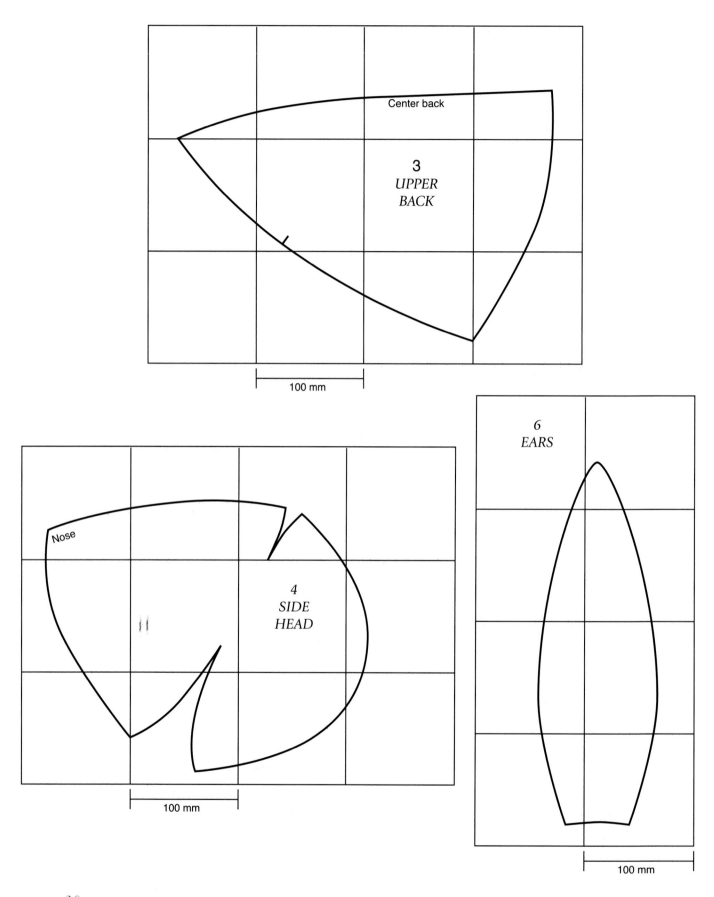

Center back

3
UPPER
BACK

100 mm

Nose

4
SIDE
HEAD

100 mm

6
EARS

100 mm

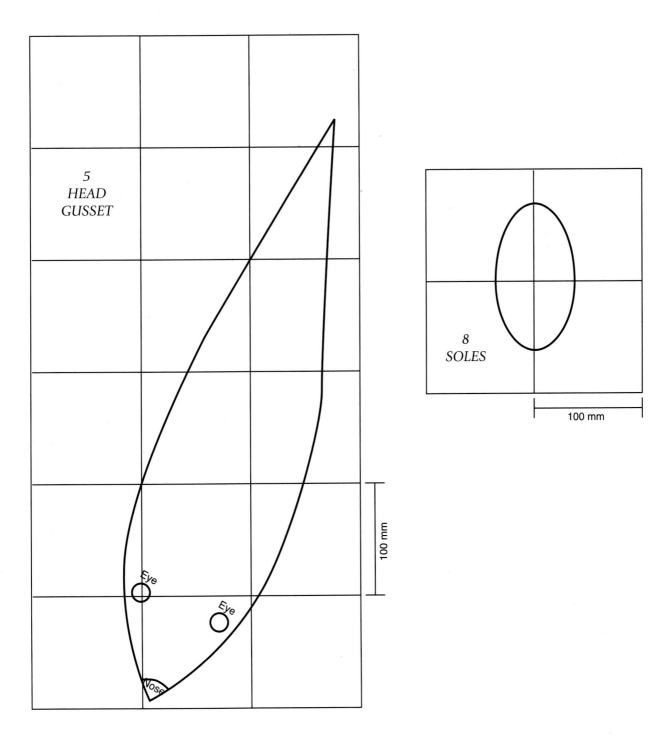

5
HEAD
GUSSET

Eye

Eye

Nose

100 mm

8
SOLES

100 mm

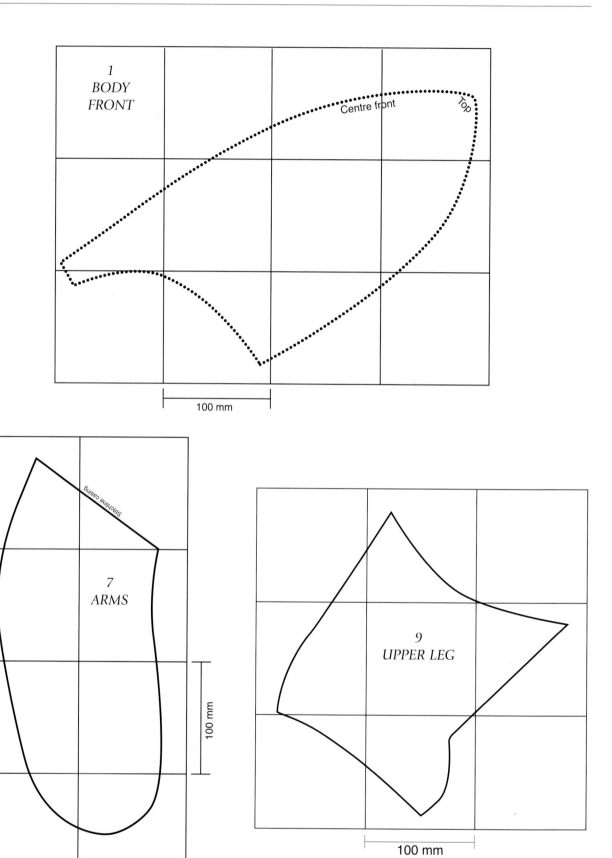

1
BODY
FRONT

Centre front

Top

100 mm

7
ARMS

Stitchline casing

100 mm

9
UPPER LEG

100 mm

Teddy Bear Quilt

It looks complicated but is so simple! This quilt is made with a purchased baby quilt panel, available at many craft stores. Choose a complementary fabric for the quilt back, cut 2.54 cm (1 in) larger all around than the quilt-top (you will turn over edges twice to bind the top). Pin the edges of the panel to a same-sized piece of synthetic batting, centre that over the wrong side of the quilt-back and baste the layers together. Hand-stitch around the motif outlines. An embroidery hoop will make this much easier. Stitch along the vertical and horizontal lines of the panel as well, to give the effect of quilting. You can use matching or contrasting sewing thread, depending on the effect you want to create.

EASY FOR THE
CHILDREN

A Tisket, a Tasket...

These baskets make wonderful gifts and the more you make, the easier they become. At Christmas, fill them with nuts and chocolates. They can be used to keep pocket money safe, or for ribbons and bows.

If you want to make a larger basket, just buy more rope and keep on wrapping.

MATERIALS

6 m (6 yd 24 in) of 6 mm (¼ in) thick sisal rope (available from hardware stores)

Safety pin, medium-sized

Scissors

50 cm (20 in) of black homespun

50 cm (20 in) of white homespun

Ruler

Masking tape

Pencil

INSTRUCTIONS

1 Taper one end of the rope with the scissors so that the three coils that make up the rope are separated and at three different lengths (see picture 1).

2 Tape the tapered end with

Tapering the rope

Beginning to wrap the rope at one end

Use a joining stitch to match the pattern

masking tape from about 10 cm (4 in) down, wrapping it around and around the rope, making sure the end is well covered. Set it aside.

3 Measure along the shortest side of both the black and white homespun fabrics, making a mark every 3 cm (1 ⅛ in). Cut a small nick at each mark with the scissors, then, at every nick, rip the fabric all the way down the length of the fabric. Pull off any fraying bits and make two piles of fabric beside you, one black and one white.

4 Fasten the safety pin at the very end of one of the white fabric strips. Pick up the rope and wrap the other end of the fabric around the masking tape starting about 10 cm (4 in) from the end of the rope and working back; wrap the fabric over the end point, then start working back up the rope (see picture 2). Each wrap should just cover the last so that no rope is showing. After five wraps along the rope, fold the end piece over into a tight coil shape and wrap the fabric over two adjoining pieces of rope to hold them together, using the safety pin like a needle.

5 When you run out of white fabric, start the black fabric by overlapping one wrap of the last piece of the fabric; do not start a new colour at a joining wrap.

6 Now you can start working your basket. Wrap the fabric three times around the rope, always working away form you, pulling tight each time, then pushing the safety pin through the last row of rope just worked. Wrap it around, pushing the safety pin up over the middle of the joining stitch and back to the start again (see picture 3). This joining stitch holds your work together.

7 Make five complete rounds of the basket-not counting the centre coil. Turn the circular base sideways and continue working in the same fashion, only working from the side and laying your first round of rope directly on top of the last round on the bottom to form an edge. Do a joining stitch every three wraps of fabric and you will start to see a pattern forming. Work six or seven rows up the side, pulling the basket into a round shape as you go.

TO FINISH
When the side is completed, you must taper the end of the rope as you did at the beginning. Finish by wrapping the fabric over the end a couple of times and going into the row below to tie it down. Tuck the fabric inside the basket, making a knot over one of the joining stitches. If this part is not securely tied, the basket will come undone.

FOR THE LID
You can have an open basket, finishing it off by tying a bow over the last stitch worked, or you might like to add a lid. The lid is worked in exactly the same way as the base of the basket with the same number of rounds. When the lid is the right size, finish it off in the same way as the basket, tapering the end with masking tape as before. To attach the lid you can either tie a bow across the last stitch, joining it to the basket at the same time, or you can just go over the basket and lid together, finishing off on the inside of the basket.

Dolly Quilt

Every little girl will love this quilt to wrap her favourite dolly in.

MATERIALS

Twelve small pieces of different cotton fabrics

24 cm x 30 cm (9 ½ in x 12 in) of cotton fabric for the backing

21 cm x 27 cm (8 ⅜ in x 10 ⅝ in) of wadding

Four tea bags

Large saucepan

Embroidery thread, cream

Ordinary sewing cotton

Scissors

Pins

Pencil

Tracing paper

Size 7 needle

Cardboard

Iron

INSTRUCTION

See the pattern on page 37.

CUTTING

1 Trace the square pattern and cut it out. Copy it onto the cardboard and cut it out again.

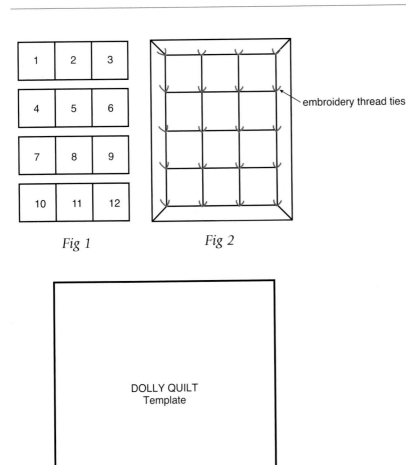

Fig 1

Fig 2

embroidery thread ties

DOLLY QUILT
Template

2 Place the cardboard square on the back of the twelve different fabrics. Draw around the squares, then cut them out, adding a 1 cm (³⁄₈ in) seam allowance around each square when you cut. The pencil line is where you will sew.

SEWING
The squares are sewn together two at a time and you will need to pin them together first. Then, with the ordinary sewing cotton and using running stitch, sew the squares together in rows of three in the order shown in Fig. 1. Then sew the four rows together two at a time to make the two halves of

the quilt. Finally, stitch the two halves together. Start and end all your sewing with a back stitch and make sure you always have the right sides together before you start. If you have sewn exactly along the pencil line then the squares will fit neatly, one on top of the other.

TEA-DYING
Carefully fill the saucepan with boiling water and pop in the four tea bags. Stir the tea bags around a few times, then place the finished top and the backing fabric into the sauce-pan. Stir, then leave them there for ten minutes. Lift the fabrics

out of the tea with a pair of tongs and wash them under a cold water tap. Squeeze them and hang them out to dry. When they are nearly dry, iron them flat, pressing all the seams to one side, and your squares will have an instant 'aged' look.

ASSEMBLING
1 Place the top piece with the right side facing you, in the middle of the wadding then place them both on top of the backing fabric which is right side down. Turn the edges of the backing fabric over onto the top, making a border. Pin all three layers together.

2 When you reach the corner, fold one fabric under the other so that the corners are neatly tucked in. Sew around the border in a small running stitch with two strands of embroidery thread. You don't have to hem the edge, this adds to its 'aged' look. Finish your sewing on the back with a back stitch.

TO FINISH
This quilt is tied to hold the wadding firmly in place. Take two strands of embroidery thread and tie each corner by taking the thread from the front of your work (you won't need a knot) taking it all the way through to the back and coming up again in the same spot on the front. Pull the thread through until it's about 4 cm (1 ⁵⁄₈ in) long and then tie four tight knots. Cut the other side of the thread the same length. Do this on every corner (Fig. 2).

The Ragamuffins

MATERIALS

For the black doll

25 cm (10 in) of black homespun

25 cm (10 in) of fabric for the dress

Two buttons for the eyes

8-ply black wool for the hair

Embroidery thread: red, black

Ordinary sewing cotton, black

For the white doll

25 cm (10 in) of white homespun

25 cm (10 in) of fabric for the dress

Small piece of fabric for the apron

Two buttons for the eyes

Cream mohair wool for the hair

Embroidery thread: red, white

Ordinary sewing cotton, white

1 m (40 in) of pink ribbon

38 cm (15 in) of cream lace

Tapestry needle

For both

Cardboard

Pencil tracing paper

Scissors

Pinking shears

Pins

Size 7 needle

Stuffing

INSTRUCTIONS

See the patterns on pages 41–43

For the black doll

1 Trace the pattern on page 41. Cut out the tracing and copy it onto the cardboard. Cut the pattern piece out of the cardboard.

2 Fold the black homespun over so it is doubled. Place the pattern on the right side of the homespun and draw around the shape. Mark the opening on the leg with the pencil. With the pinking shears, cut out around the doll 1 cm (⅜ in) from the pencil line. The pencil line is where you will sew.

3 Pink the two pieces together around the outside edge then, with two strands of black embroidery thread and starting with a strong back stitch, sew along the pencil line with small running stitches. Begin at one side of the opening mark and finish at the other side of the mark with a back stitch. Do not cut off the thread, but leave it hanging.

4 Take some stuffing and gently push it into the head and outer arm first-a little at a time-until the doll is firmly stuffed. Now sew up the opening with the hanging thread and do a strong back stitch to finish. Trim the edge if needed.

For the dress

1 Make a cardboard pattern for the dress as for the doll. Fold the dress material over double with the right sides together. Place the pattern on the fabric with the shoulder part on the fold. Cut out the dress, leaving a 1 cm (⅜ in) seam allowance. Cut the bottom of the dress with pinking shears.

2 Pin the two sides and the arm seams, then stitch with the ordinary cotton in a small running stitch. End with a back stitch. Turn the dress the right way out.

3 With two strands of embroidery thread and a running stitch, start on the inside neck and stitch around the opening, about 5 mm (¼ in) from the edge. When you get back to the beginning knot, pop the dress over the doll's head and pull the thread up tightly around the doll's neck. Do two back stitches to hold it tight and hide your thread under the dress. The sleeves are sewn in exactly the same way.

For the hair

1 Mark the five positions for the hair on the doll's head and cut five pieces of homespun, each 2 cm x 10 cm (¾ in x 4 in). Fold each piece in half and pin the middle of it to one of the marks on the head. Sew on each piece with a back stitch going over the same spot five times.

2 Cut the black wool into five bundles of ten 10 cm (4 in) lengths of wool each. Place these in the middle of the homespun strips and tie them into a firm knot (Fig. 1). Make sure the knot is tied tightly or the wool will fall out.

TO FINISH

Sew on two buttons for the eyes, using the tie method and the red embroidery thread. For the mouth, push your needle in from the back and sew a cross, then take your thread to the back again and do a back stitch. You might like to draw

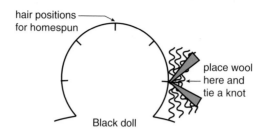

hair positions for homespun

place wool here and tie a knot

Black doll

Fig 1

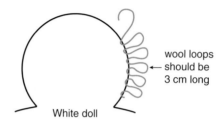

wool loops should be 3 cm long

White doll

Fig 2

the mouth on in pencil first, so you know where to sew.

For the white doll

Follow steps 1–4 as for the black doll, using the white homespun and white cotton.

For the dress

1 Make the dress is the same way as for the black doll. Pin the cream lace to the bottom of the doll's dress, then stitch it in a running stitch in ordinary cotton. Overlap the lace slightly where the ends meet and finish off the stitching on the inside.

2 Trace the apron pattern and draw it onto cardboard as before. Fold the apron over

double and place the pattern on the doubled fabric with the shoulders on the fold line. Cut out the apron with ordinary scissors. Make a mark where the ribbon ties will go on each side. Cut four pieces of ribbon, each 18 cm (7 in) long. Back stitch one end of each one to the marks on the apron. Pop the apron over the dress and tie the ribbons on each side in a big bow.

For the hair

Cut a long length of the mohair wool and put a knot in one end. You will need to use the tapestry needle for this part. Starting at the base of the head, do a loose overstitch all

the way around the head (Fig. 2). The hair should stand out about 3 cm (1 ⅛ in) from the head-don't pull your thread tightly, just stitch slowly in and out, leaving 3 cm loose each time you do a stitch. When you reach the end, do a back stitch carefully without pulling the other stitches. The mohair gives a nice 'woolly' look to the hair, and the rough texture of the wool will stop it from slipping. I would not recommend a smooth wool for this type of stitch.

Finish as for the black doll.

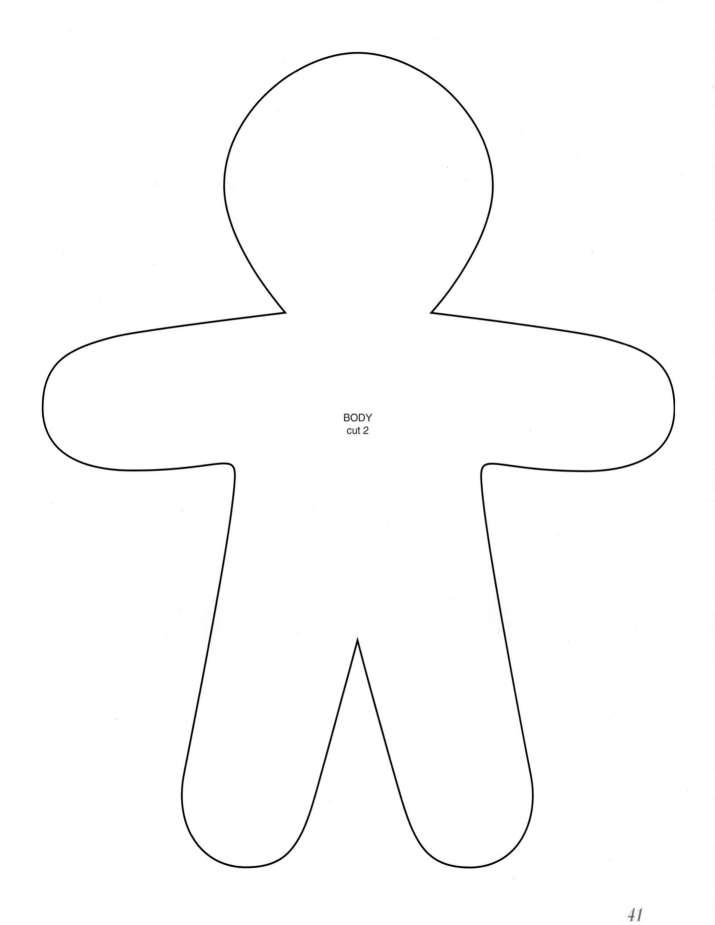

BODY
cut 2

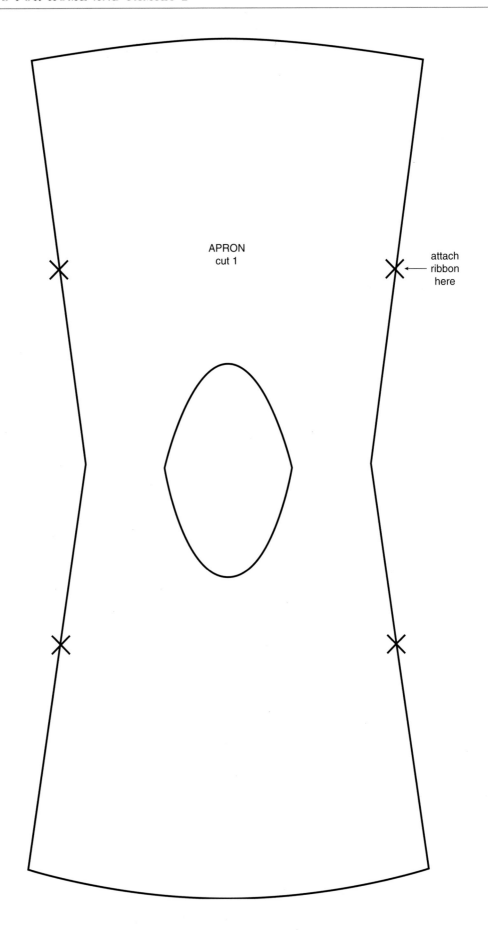

APRON
cut 1

attach
ribbon
here

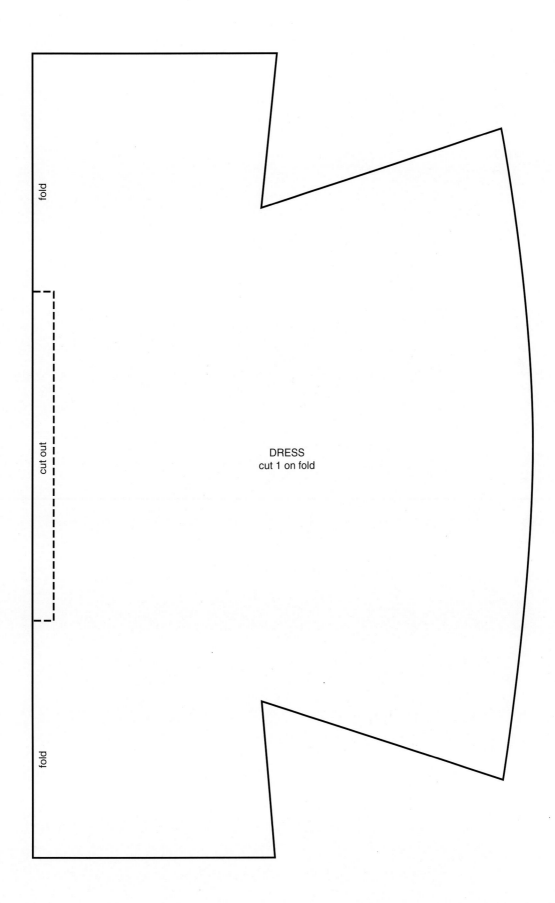

fold

cut out

fold

DRESS
cut 1 on fold

SOFT FURNISHINGS

Cushions

General instructions for making cushions

OPENINGS AND CLOSURES

A cushion cover needs to be fully removable for laundering. Zippers are the most common way to close cushion covers; however, Velcro, buttons and ties are all suitable.

The placement of the opening may vary. A back vent in the middle of the back of the cushion cover is often used when the cushion does not need to be turned over. A side vent opening is concealed in a side seam so that the cushion cover can be reversible.

Decorative items, such as buttons and bows, provide added interest as well as providing a functional method for opening and closing.

BACK VENT OPENING

1 Cut the cushion cover form to the finished size plus 1.5 cm (⅝ in) all around for seam allowances. Cut out a cushion cover back to the same size, but add 11 cm (4 ⅜ in) to two opposite sides to form a rectangle. Cut the rectangle in half across the long sides; these cut edges will be the centre back edges.

2 Turn in and press 1.5 cm (⅝ in) to the wrong side along the centre back edges, then turn in and press another 1.5 cm (⅝ in). Stitch.

3 Place the centre back edges together so the hemmed edges overlap by 5 cm (2 in) to form the back vent. Baste these edges together.

4 Complete the cushion cover as described in the instructions for the cushion you have chosen.

VELCRO CLOSURE

1 Cut the cushion cover front to the finished size plus 1.5 cm (⅝ in) seam allowances all around. Cut out a cushion cover back to the same size, but add 11 cm (4 ⅜ in) to two opposite sides to form a rectangle. Cut the rectangle in half across the long sides; these cut edges will be the centre back edges.

2 Turn in and press 1.5 cm (⅝ in) to the wrong side along the centre back edges, then turn in and press another 1.5 cm (⅝ in). Stitch.

3 Pin one half of the Velcro strip on to the right side of one half of the cushion cover back, over the hem just stitched. Test the closure to ensure the back will close in a perfect square before stitching the Velcro into place.

4 Complete the cushion cover as described in the instructions for the cushion you have chosen.

BUTTONS

1 Cut the cushion cover front to the finished size plus 1.5 cm (⅝ in) seam allowances all around. Cut out a cushion cover back to the same size, but add 11 cm (4 ⅜ in) to two opposite sides to form a rectangle. Cut the rectangle in half across the long sides; these cut edges will be the centre back edges.

2 Turn in and press 1.5 cm (⅝ in) to the wrong side along the centre back edges, then turn in and press another 1.5 cm (⅝ in) Stitch.

3 Mark the positions for the buttons and buttonholes on the two hems just stitched.

4 Make the buttonholes on the top half of the opening and sew the buttons to the right side of the bottom half.

5 Complete the cushion cover as described in the instructions for the cushion you have chosen.

BOWS OR TIES

In addition to your main fabric, you will need to allow approximately 6 cm x 20 cm (2 ⅜ in x 8 in) fabric for each tie. These can be cut on the bias or on the grain.

1 Decide how many pairs of ties you need and cut out the required pieces.

2 For each tie, fold the fabric strip over double with the right sides together and the raw edges even. Sew down the long side and one end. Turn the tie through to the right side. Press.

3 Cut out a cushion cover front and a cushion cover back with a 1.5 cm (⅝ in) seam allowance all around. Pin the raw ends of the ties on to the right side of the cushion cover back and front, so that the raw ends of the ties match the raw edge of the cushion cover.

4 Cut two pieces of fabric for the facings, each 5 cm (2 in) wide by the width of the cushion. Place one facing piece on each half of the cushion cover over the ties with the right sides facing and with the raw edge of the facing matching the raw edge of the cushion cover on the opening edge. Stitch along the opening edge. Turn the facing to the wrong side. Press.

5 Complete the cushion cover as described in the instructions for the cushion you have chosen.

ZIPPERS

Inserting a centred zipper

1 Measure and mark on the opening the length of the zipper teeth plus 5 mm (¼ in). Close the zipper seam with a basting stitch and press the seam open.

2 Open the zipper and position it face down on the seam allowance so that the zipper teeth are along the seam line. Baste the zipper into place along one side of the zipper tape. Close the zipper and baste the other side into place.

3 Turn the fabric right side up with the zipper underneath. Using the zipper foot on your sewing machine and commencing at the top of the zipper, stitch down one side, then across the bottom of the zipper and back up to the top. Remove the basting stitches.

Lapped zipper in a piped seam

1 Press the seam allowance of the opening under, along the seam line.

2 With the piped pieces together, lay it face down over the seam allowance with the zipper teeth resting on the top of the piping.

3 Baste along the zipper tape close to the zipper teeth. Check that the zipper will open and close smoothly, before stitching it in place. Remove the basting.

Offset zipper

This method is used to conceal a zipper from view.

1 With the zipper open, position it over the opening so that the zipper teeth are centred over the right-hand seam allowance. Baste one side of the tape into position 5 mm (¼ in) from the zipper teeth.

2 Close the zipper and baste the other side of the zipper to the other seam allowance.

3 Turn the fabric right side up and topstitch the zipper in place through all the layers of fabric, using the zipper foot on your sewing machine and stitching close to the ends of the zipper. Remove the basting.

BINDING

Making continuous bias binding

1 Cut a piece of bias fabric (Fig. 1). Decide on the width of your bias strip, including seam allowances, and mark the bias strips as shown.

2 Fold the fabric with the right sides together, so that both points A and both points B are matching. Note that one strip width extends on each side. Join AA to BB with a 5 mm (¼ in) seam. Press the seam open. Cut along the marked line for the bias strip (Fig. 2).

Making and joining strips of bias binding

1 To find the bias on a piece of fabric, fold in one corner so that the top edge is parallel to the selvage. Press the fold. This pressed line is the bias. Draw in lines parallel to the pressed line, the desired width of the bias strip apart. Cut along these lines.

2 Join two strips by placing one length of bias right side up and the second length of fabric wrong side up across each other at an angle of 45 degrees, with the raw edges matching at the end (Fig. 3).

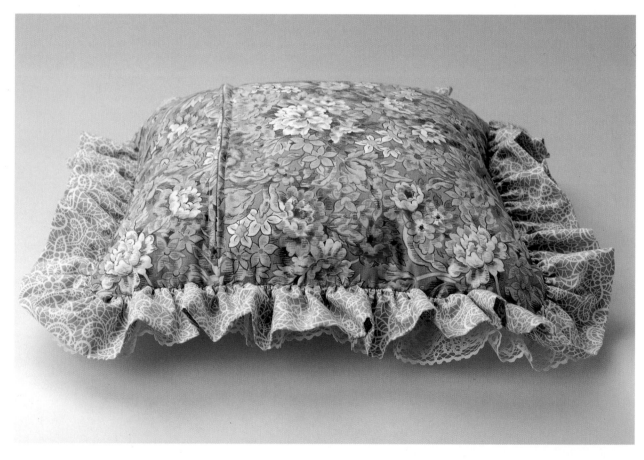

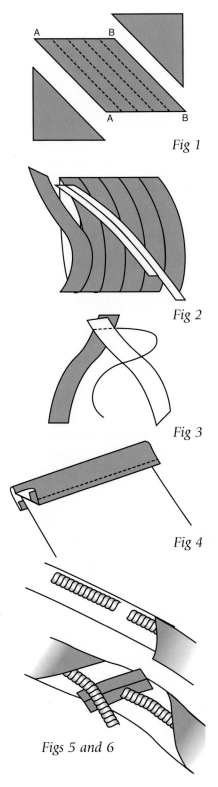

Fig 1

Fig 2

Fig 3

Fig 4

Figs 5 and 6

3 Stitch the ends together as shown. Press the seam open.

Attaching the binding

Fold the bias strip in half lengthways with the wrong sides facing and place it over both raw edges of the seam. If you are using bias binding you have made yourself, you will need to fold the raw edges under before you pin it in position. Pin and stitch the bias strip into place inside the seam allowance, catching both sides of the bias in the seam (Fig. 4).

PIPING

To make piping

1 Make the required length of continuous bias binding. Remember, the bias strip must be wide enough to wrap around the piping cord, leaving sufficient seam allowances on both sides for the stitching.

2 Measure the length of piping you require for your project. Cords can be joined, if necessary, by butting two ends together and binding them with matching thread or by carefully intertwining the strands (Figs. 5 and 6).

3 Fold the bias strip over the piping cord. Using matching sewing thread and the zipper foot on your sewing machine, stitch through both sides of the bias strip, stitching close to the cord.

Attaching piping

1 With the right side of one fabric piece facing upwards, lay the piping on top so that the raw edges of the binding match with the raw edge of the fabric and the covered cord lies on the fabric. Baste into position.

2 Place the other piece of fabric right side down, over the top of the other fabric and piping, again using the zipper foot and stitching close to the cord. If necessary, trim the seam allowances to remove any excess bulk.

3 Fold the fabrics right side out with the piping fixed securely between the layers of fabric.

FRILLS AND RUFFLES

Frills and ruffles are one of the easiest decorating finishes for a variety of soft furnishing projects.

Making a ruffle

1 Cut out a strip for the ruffle, adding 3 cm (1 ⅛ in) for the bottom hem. If you need to join strips to achieve the full length, add 1.5 cm (⅝ in) for each joining seam allowance.

2 Double hem the bottom edge of the ruffle. To gather the ruffle, handsew or machine-sew two parallel rows of gathering stitches across the raw edge in the seam allowance.

Applying an even ruffle

There is a technique to ensure that the ruffling looks even on your finished project.

1 Marking with pins, divide the length of the ruffle into equal parts and then divide the edge to which it will be applied into the same number of equal parts. For smaller projects, four divisions are usual, but for larger projects and circles, six equal parts may be required. If you are attaching the ruffle to a cushion, use the four corners as your marks.

2 Pin the ruffle on, matching the pin marks and adjusting the gathering evenly between them. Pin and baste, then stitch the ruffle into place.

Basic piped cushion

MATERIALS

40 cm (16 in) square of fabric for the cushion cover front

Two pieces of fabric, each 22 cm x 40 cm (8 ¾ in x 16 in) for the cushion cover backs

40 cm (16 in) square cushion insert

30 cm (12 in) zipper

1.7 m (68 in) of corded piping (see how to make and apply piping on page 49)

Matching sewing thread

Scissors

Pins

Tape measure

Sewing machine

An interesting fabric, such as this one, needs only very simple trimming to make an attractive cushion.

METHOD

1 Place the two 40 cm (16 in) edges of the back pieces together with the right sides facing and the raw edges even. Stitch a 5 cm (2 in) long seam at each end, leaving an opening in the centre for the zipper. Insert the zipper. Open the zipper to allow for turning the cushion cover.

2 With right sides facing and the raw edges matching, pin the piping around the edge of the cushion cover front, clipping the piping seam allowances at the corners to allow it to curve gently. Cut 2 cm (¾ in) of the piping cord

out of one end of the piping to lessen the bulk at the overlap. Overlap the piping ends. Sew on the piping using the zipper foot on your sewing machine and stitching as close as possible to the piping.

3 Pin and baste the cushion cover back and cushion cover front together with the right sides facing and all the raw edges matching. Stitch around all sides, stitching in the piping stitching line. Trim the seams and clip the corners.

4 Turn the cushion cover right side out through the zipper opening. Remove any basting stitches that are visible. Press.

Frilled piped cushion

MATERIALS

40 cm (16 in) square of fabric for the cushion cover front

Two pieces of fabric, each 22 cm x 40 cm (8 ¾ in x 16 in) for the cushion cover back

1.7 m (68 in) of contrasting piping

30 cm (12 in) zipper

3.2 m (3 ½ yd) fabric strip for the ruffle

40 cm (16 in) square cushion insert

Matching sewing machine thread

A contrasting ruffle makes a strong decorative statement.

Simple trimmings, cleverly applied, make a plain cushion into a unique one.

Scissors

Pins

Tape measure

Sewing machine

METHOD

1 Make a two-colour ruffle as instructed on page 49. Make the piping as instructed on page 49 or purchase ready-made piping.

2 With the right sides of the fabric facing and the raw edges matching, sew the piping and then the completed ruffle around the edge of the cushion cover front. If you are attaching the ruffle separately, after the piping, sew in the piping stitching line.

3 Place the two 40 cm (16 in) edges of the back pieces together with the right sides facing and the raw edges even. Stitch a 5 cm (2 in) long seam at each end, leaving an opening in the centre for the zipper. Insert the zipper. Open the zipper to allow for turning the cushion cover to the right side.

4 Place the cushion cover back and front together with the right sides facing and the raw edges following the piping stitching line. Trim the seams and clip the corners to reduce the bulk. Turn the cushion cover to the right side through the zipper opening and press.

Cushion with contrast band

MATERIALS

40 cm (16 in) square of fabric for the cushion cover front

Two pieces of fabric, each 22 cm x 40 cm (8 ¾ in x 16 in) for the cushion cover back

Four strips of border fabric, each 5 cm x 32 cm (2 in x 12 ¾ in)

1.7 m (68 in) of contrasting corded piping (see how to make corded piping on page 49)

30 cm (12 in) zipper

40 cm (16 in) square cushion insert

Matching sewing machine thread

Scissors

Pins

Tape measure

Sewing machine

METHODS

1 Trim the short ends of the border strips to perfect diagonals (Fig. 1). Join the strips with mitred corners to form a square (Fig. 1) which fits the cushion cover, 4 cm from the outside edge, as shown. Clip in 1 cm (⅜ in) on the inner corner seams. Press the seams open.

2 Press under 1 cm (⅜ in) on the inside and outside edges of the square. Pin the square on to the cushion cover front. Edgestitch into place. Press.

3 Attach the piping to the cushion cover front. Insert the zipper into the cushion cover back as instructed on page 47.

4 Place the cushion cover front and cushion cover back together with the right sides facing and the raw edges matching. Stitch around the

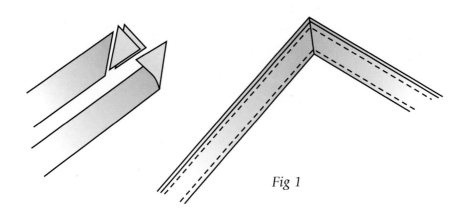

Fig 1

This triangular cushion with its bright contrasting piping is the perfect partner for the checked slipcover.

outside edge. Trim excess bulk from the corners and seams. Turn the cushion cover to the right side through the zipper opening. Press.

Machine-appliqued cushion

MATERIALS

Fabric, featuring flowers, animals, borders or any motif that will lend itself to being cut out

30 cm (12 in) square of fabric for the cushion cover front

Two pieces of fabric, each 17 cm x 30 cm (6 ¾ in x 12 in), for the cushion cover backs

12 cm x 2.4 m (4 ¾ in x 2 yd 24 in) fabric strip for the ruffle

Four strips of border fabric, each 5 cm x 32 cm (2 in x 12 ¾ in)

1.7 m (68 in) of contrasting corded piping (see how to make corded piping on page 49)

25 cm (10 in) zipper

30 cm (12 in) square cushion insert

Fusible interfacing (optional)

Matching sewing machine thread

Scissors

Pins

Sewing machine

Warm iron

Pressing cloth

METHOD

1 Cut out around the motif, leaving a 2 cm (¾ in) margin all around. Interface the motif if necessary. Pin or baste the motif on the area to be appliquéd.

2 Zigzag around the motif

5 mm (¼ in) in from the cut edge. Trim away the excess fabric, close to the stitching. Stitch again over the first zigzag stitching, using a slightly wider satin stitch.

3 Join the short ends of the ruffle strip. Fold the ruffle over double with wrong sides together and raw edges matching. Press. Gather the raw edges together. Apply the ruffle to the cushion front as instructed on page 49.

4 Insert the zipper into the cushion cover back as instructed on page 47, remembering to leave the zipper open.

5 Place the cushion cover back on the front, with the right sides facing. Stitch around the outside edge, through all thicknesses, following the piping stitching line. Turn the cushion cover to the right side through the zipper opening and press.

Triangular cushion

BEFORE YOU BEGIN

You can make a triangular insert for this cushion from calico, following these instructions but omitting the zipper; or simply stuff the cushion cover with polyester fibrefill.

MATERIALS

60 cm (24 in) of 140 cm (56 in) wide fabric

2.6 m (2 yd 32 in) of 6 cm (2 ⅜ in) wide contrasting bias binding

2.6 m (2 yd 32 in) of piping cord

Matching sewing machine thread

30 cm (12 in) zipper

Polyester fibrefill

Scissors

Pins

Tape measure

Sewing machine

METHOD

1 Cut out two triangles with each side measuring 42 cm (16 ¾ in) including a 1.5 cm (⅝ in) seam allowance.

2 Make two lengths of piping, each one 130 cm (52 in). (See page 49.)

3 Cut a piece of fabric for the wall, 13 cm x 129 cm (5 ⅛ in x 51 ½ in) including seam allowances. If you need to join lengths to achieve the total length, add 1.5 cm (⅝ in) for seam allowances on joining seams.

4 Pin the piping around the right side of the top and bottom pieces with raw edges matching and the right sides together. Clip into the seam allowance of the piping to allow it to curve around the corners. Overlap the piping as neatly as possible at the ends, pulling the ends into the seam allowances. Stitch.

5 To attach the wall, pin and baste the ends of the strip together to form a circle. Check the fit. You may have to make a slight adjustment. Pin the wall to the top cushion piece with the right sides facing and the raw edges even. Stitch in the piping stitching line. Trim the seam allowance.

6 Stitch the wall to the bottom cushion piece in the same way as for the top, leaving a 30 cm

For a fresh country look, stencil calico with farmyard motifs.

(12 in) opening along one side for the zipper. Trim any excess bulk around the corners and at the seams.

7 Insert the zipper and leave it open. (See page 47 for how to insert a zipper.) Turn the cushion to the right side through the open zipper and press.

8 Stuff the cushion firmly and evenly with the fibrefill, ensuring that the corners are well filled. Close the zipper.

Stencilled cushion

MATERIALS

Firm plastic sheet for the stencil

Fineline marker pen

Sharp craft knife or scalpel

Bread board or similar cutting board

Stencil brushes

Paints

Masking tape

Fabric for practice and testing colours

Fabric and notions for creating the cushion of your choice

METHOD

1 Place the plastic sheet over the motif and trace around the design, using the marker pen. Cut the stencil out on the cutting board, using the sharp knife or scalpel. Remember to leave 'bridges' in the design that are not cut through.

2 Place the stencil on the cushion cover front. Define the

The stencils above and on next page provide a basic outline. Change any detail to please yourself.

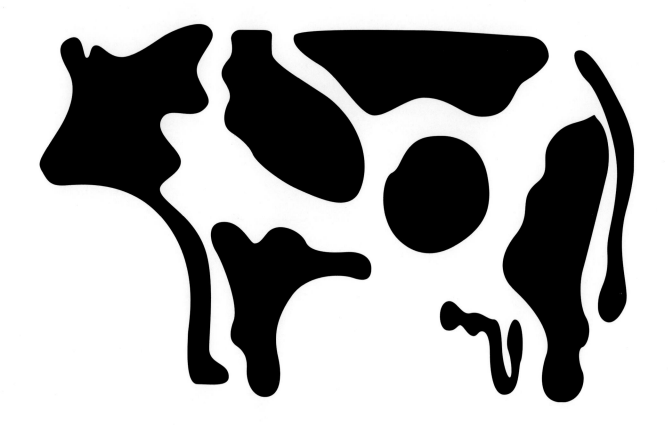

stencil areas that will be the same colour by covering all other areas with masking tape. Taking care to paint the elements in their logical order (main colour first, then details), start stencilling from the outside, gradually filling in the entire area until you are happy with the depth of colour. Each time you finish stencilling a colour, you can cover it with tape and uncover the next area to be painted. It is a good idea to let each section of colour dry before you begin applying the next one, to avoid them bleeding into one another. Allow all the paint to dry before you begin sewing.

3 Make up your cushion using any of the methods already described.

Re-embroidered chintz cushion

This cushion is shaped to suit the motif. We have used fabrics and colours to trim the ruffle that complement the chintz. Make your cushion in the one fabric, big or small, or with a simple contrasting piping if you prefer. Whichever method you choose you are sure to have some very original embroideries.

STITCHES

The design of your fabric will suggest the best stitches to use in embroidering. Generally, the stems and fine vein lines are best worked in tiny chain stitches, either in lines, or in curled 'snail shell' circles to fill in the larger areas. Work petals and other broad areas of colour in long and short stitch. This gives you the opportunity to subtly vary the tones of colour, by shading them across the area. French knots are ideal for small dots, or even for filling in the centre of a flower, as the texture from grouped French knots is very attractive. Stem stitch, back stitch and satin stitch are also worth considering and simple blanket stitch is effective for outlining a flower.

All these stitches are outlined in the stitch guide on page 206. Work with an embroidery hoop to make your stitching easier and to prevent distortion of the fabric. Try to match closely the colour of the embroidery thread to the

colour of your motif — the purpose of this type of embroidery is to embellish and add texture to the design, not to draw attention to any particular stitch.

MATERIALS

Sufficient chintz fabric for the cushion front, border, cushion back and frill

Sufficient contrasting fabric for the frill

Sufficient 2.54 cm (1 in) wide toning bias binding to go around the embroidered panel

Stranded embroidery cotton in the colours of your choice

Matching sewing thread

Zipper

A cushion insert (purchased cushion insert or one made to measure)

METHOD

Make your cushion any size and shape that complements your fabric. Remember, your embroidered panel will be about 9 cm (3 ½ in) smaller than the finished cushion.

1 Re-embroider the centre panel of your cushion in the stitches described above. When the embroidery is complete, turn under the outside edges of the panel and press.

2 Press open sufficient 2.54 cm (1 in) wide toning bias binding. Fold it over double lengthways with right sides together. Press. Pin this bias binding under the edge of the embroidered panel so that the folded edge just protrudes. Overlap the two raw ends and then tuck them neatly out of sight under the embroidered panel. Baste.

3 Cut a piece of fabric the same shape as the embroidered panel but about 10 cm (4 in) larger all around. Place the embroidered panel onto the centre of the larger piece, taking care that the border is the same size all around. Stitch through all thicknesses around the embroidered panel.

4 Measure around the edge of the cushion front and cut two and a half times this amount of 10 cm (4 in) wide fabric for the frill. Cut another identical length 12 cm (4 ¾ in) wide from a contrasting fabric. Join these two strips together along one long edge with right sides facing. Join the short ends, with right sides together, to form a continuous circle. Fold the circular strip over double with wrong sides together so that the raw edges are even and press. You should have a band of contrasting fabric at the outer edge of your frill strip. If your cushion is square, mark the frill strip into quarters. Gather up the frill, starting and stopping your gathering thread at the quarter points. Pin the frill to the right side of the cushion front, placing the quarter points to the corners of the cushion front and having the raw edges even. Adjust the gathers to fit. If your cushion is oblong, mark halfway points along the long sides of the cushion front and mark the frill into two parts. Gather the frill, starting and stopping your gathering thread at the halfway points. Pin the frill around the right side of the cushion front, matching these two points and having the raw edges even, adjust the gathers to fit.

5 Cut two back pieces, each one the same length as the front but half the width plus 3 cm (1 ⅛ in). Join these pieces in a 3 cm (1 ⅛ in) seam, leaving an opening in the centre for the zipper. Insert zipper and leave it open.
6 Fold the frill towards the centre of the embroidered

panel. Place the cushion back over the frilled front panel with right sides facing and raw edges matching. Stitch around the outside edge, following the stitching line for the frill and taking care not to catch the frill as you sew. Turn the cushion to the right side through the zipper opening.

If a commercial cushion insert is not available in a size to suit your cushion, make a calico bag the size of your cushion leaving an opening to insert polyester fibre stuffing or feathers. Once the cushion insert is filled, handsew the opening closed.

Director's Chairs

Director's chairs have found a place in many households. Reasonably priced, comfortable and easy to store, they can undergo endless transformations.

Director's chair 1

MEASURING
Starting at the front of your chair at ground level, measure the distance up to the seat plus the depth of the seat up to the top of the chair back plus the distance from the top of the chair, then back to ground level. Record the measurement for the depth of the seat and the width of the back rest separately. Measure from the ground level up to and over each arm rest down to the seat. Add 1.5 cm (⅝ in) seam allowances to all measurements. Make rough drawings, marking in these measurements.

MATERIALS
Pencil and paper
Approximately 2.8 m (112 in) of 120 cm (48 in) wide fabric
30 cm (12 in) of contrasting fabric for the ties
Matching sewing machine thread
Scissors
Tape measure
Pins
Sewing machine

A bold check cotton slipcover gives new life to an old chair.

1 Using your drawings as a guide, cut out the three pattern pieces. Cut four 15 cm (6 in) wide ties, each 40 cm (16 in) long.

2 Do not remove the existing seat or backrest; the slipcover will clip over the top. Place the main pattern piece over the chair, face downwards. Do the same with each arm piece. Pin the arm pieces to the main piece at the seat level and at the front leg. Pin the front and back of the main piece together down to the arm level of the chair, finishing pinning at this point.

3 At the front of the chair, pin a dart across the top of each arm front at right angles to the front seam to ensure the drape over the arm sits straight.

4 Remove the slipcover and machine-stitch all the seams into place. Trim the excess seam allowance, if necessary.

The painted chair frame and the combination of many coordinating fabrics give this setting a decorator's touch.

Fig 1

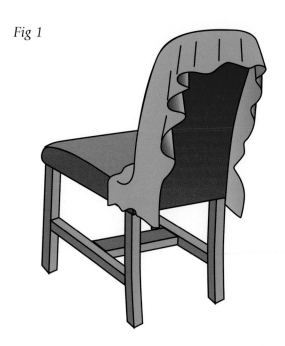

Check the fit and re-pin the darts if necessary. Mark the seam lines with tailor's chalk. Remove the back rest pieces from the chair.

4 Stitch around the top and sides, leaving a 10 cm (4 in) opening on one side of the cover.

5 Place the seat cover on the chair and pin darts in the corners to reduce the fabric bulk. Mark the seams and darts as before. Remove the seat cover from the chair. Stitch the darts, then join the inner back cover to the seat cover piece.

6 Turn in and press 5 mm (¼ in) on the bottom and the ends of the skirt, then turn and

Fig 2

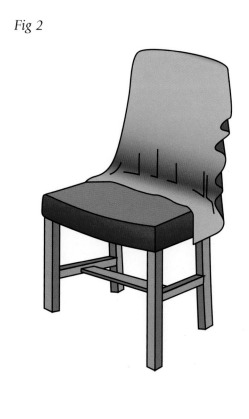

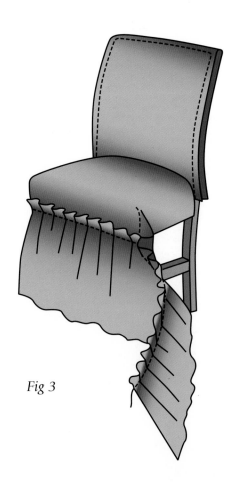

Fig 3

press another 2.54 cm (1 in). Stitch the hems in place. Divide the top edge of the skirt into quarters and mark these points with a pin. Gather the top edge of the skirt.

7 Pin the skirt to the seat cover with the right sides together and the raw edges matching, beginning and ending at one of the back corners (Fig. 3). Pull up the gathering to fit, placing a pin mark at each corner. Adjust the gathering, making it a little fuller at the corners. Stitch the skirt into place. Press.

8 Sew Velcro to the back opening to close the cover or make ties from scraps of fabric and sew them to either side of the opening.

9 If you wish to create a very charming effect, make two bows from the same fabric and slipstitch one to each side of the chair.

Tailored Chair Cover

If you have wooden dining chairs that are still solid but have seen better days, this slipcover project is an ideal refurbishing solution.

Before you begin
This easy-cover project may be the perfect opportunity to convert six odd chairs into a matched set. This slipcover pattern is designed for chairs which are flat across the top of the back rest and do not have protruding knobs-all the lines and surfaces of the chair

should be as straight as possible. Bowed backs and curved seats will not allow the fabric to hang properly. Choose your fabric carefully. You will need sturdy material that doesn't present too many problems with matching

patterns on adjacent surfaces.

Choose a contrasting or complementary fabric for the lining as it is sure to show at the joints. If you like, the slipcover can be lined with the main fabric for an all-over look. For added comfort you

Match up your odd chairs with a set of tailored slipcovers like this.

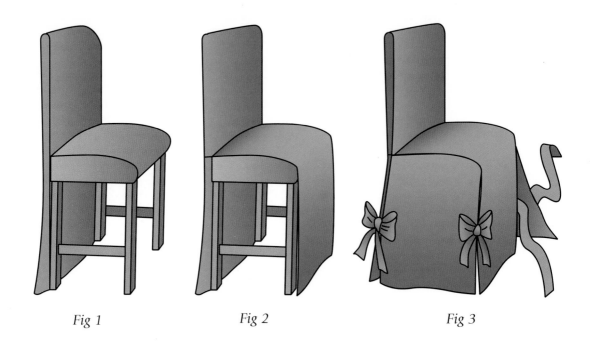

Fig 1   *Fig 2*   *Fig 3*

can include a layer of wadding between the main fabric and the lining.

MEASURING

You will need to take the measurements of your own chair then draw those rectangles onto a sheet of paper. Mark each rectangle with its position and mark all the measurements on it. The drawings here are intended as a guide only.

Pattern piece 1: Measure the length from the seat up the chair back and down to the floor (allowing for the width of the chair frame at the top of the back rest) by the width of the chair (allowing for the width of the chair frame at the side).

Pattern piece 2: Measure the depth of the seat plus the distance to the floor by the width of the chair.

Pattern piece 3: Measure the depth of the seat plus the

width of the timber frame by the height of the seat from the floor. Cut two.

Once you have established these measurements you can calculate the amount of fabric required.

MATERIALS
Sheet of paper
Pencil
Ruler
Main fabric
Lining fabric
Wadding in the same size (optional)
Matching sewing machine thread
Pins
Scissors
Tape measure
Sewing machine

METHOD

1 Cut out the pattern pieces from the main and the lining fabric, allowing 1.5 cm (⅝ in) all around for seams. Take care to match and centre any fabric pattern at this point.

2 On pattern piece 1, sew the sides together from the top of the chair back rest to the seat (Fig. 1). Press.

3 Sew pattern piece 1 to pattern piece 2 at the seat back edge (Fig. 2). Attach a pattern piece 3 at each side (Fig. 3). Press.

4 Make eight 30 cm (12 in) long ties out of scraps of the cover fabric. Pin one end of each tie, with the raw edges matching, on the right side of the fabric front and back edges, just below seat height.

5 Make the lining in the same way as for the cover. Place the lining and the cover together with the right sides facing and the raw edges even, sew around the outside edge, leaving an opening for turning, and catching the ends of the ties in the seam. Turn the cover right side out, taking care to push the corners out completely. Press.

Instant Sofa Cover-up

Instant loose covers require little sewing, only a small financial investment and not a lot of time.

Before you begin

Practise your skills by draping an old sheet on your chair or sofa. This way you will quickly be able to work out where fabric can be tucked into crevices to anchor it. If the existing sofa has torn covers and you are not likely to use it again in its present state, sew strips of Velcro to the old lounge to marry up with Velcro on the fabric to stay neatly in position and it will not crease as much.

Select a fabric, such as a linen or another woven fabric, that is less likely to show creases. Fabric bows on the arms add a further decorative touch and can be attached with Velcro, stitched or pinned into place.

You should use 137 cm (55 in) wide fabric for a two-seater sofa, as fewer joins will be necessary.

MATERIALS
Fabric
Pins
Tailor's chalk
Velcro (if required)
Cord, ribbon or sewn ties

METHOD
1 It may be necessary to join lengths of fabric together to achieve the required width. If this is the case, use flat fell seams for added strength and always carefully match the fabric pattern.

2 Remove the seat cushions. Drape and tuck the fabric piece over the base of the lounge. When you are happy with the draping, mark the hem line with tailor's chalk. Remove the cover. Even out any great irregularities in the chalk marks, then trim the excess fabric from the hem. Turn in and press a double hem. Stitch the hem in place.

3 Tie sashes, ribbons or cords around the arms to hold the fabric in place. The ties can be attached with Velcro, pins or by topstitching them into place.

Wrapped seat cushion

MATERIALS
Sufficient fabric

Pinking shears

Safety pins (optional)

Needle and thread (optional)

METHOD
1 Use pinking shears to cut out a fabric square twice the width and length of your cushion plus 30 cm (12 in). Place the cushion in the centre of the fabric, on the wrong side.

2 Wrap the cushion as if it were a present; first fold the fabric to the centre, turning in the raw edges. Secure the fabric on the underside with safety pins or stitches (Figs. 1–3 opposite).

No-sew cushion

MATERIALS
Pinking shears

METHOD
1 Cut with pinking shears, a rectangle of fabric three times the width of your cushion and twice as wide (Fig. 4 opposite).

2 Fold the fabric as indicated in the illustration, bringing both ends up to tie in a knot at the top of the cushion (Fig. 5). Place the knot to the underside for a tailored look (Fig. 6).

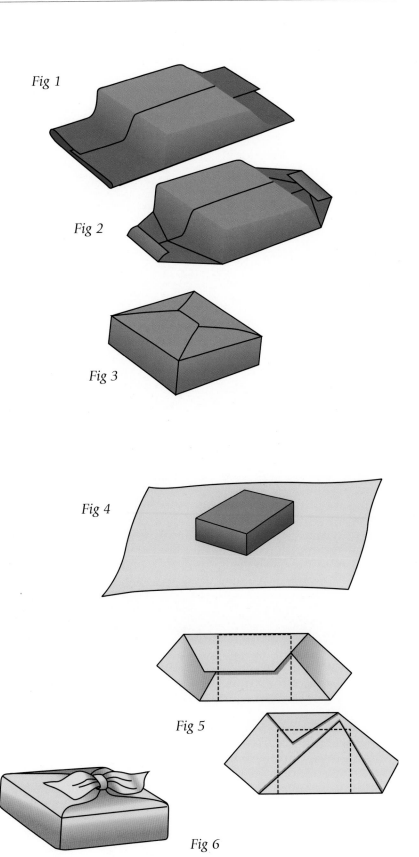

Fig 1

Fig 2

Fig 3

Fig 4

Fig 5

Fig 6

Appliquéd Linen Napery

MATERIALS

Piece of fabric, 40 cm x 60 cm (16 in x 24 in) for the basic placemat

60 cm (24 in) square of fabric for the basic napkin

Fabric motifs for the appliqué

Matching sewing machine thread

Pins

Scissors

Tailor's chalk

Tape measure

Sewing machine

METHOD

1 Cut out the motifs, allowing a 6 mm (¼ in) excess around them.

2 Position the motifs on the placemat and napkin. Baste them in place. Machine-stitch around the edge of each motif, 6 mm (¼ in) from the edge, using a small zigzag stitch. Cut away the excess fabric close to the stitching.

3 Adjust your sewing machine stitch to a wider satin stitch. Stitch again over the previous stitching, enclosing the raw edge as you stitch.

4 Make a narrow double hem around all sides of the placemat and napkin. Press.

Fringed Napery

Uneven weave fabrics, including linens and loosely woven cottons, provide the base to create interesting yet very simple table napkins and cloths with fringed edges.

Before you begin

Measure the size of your table. Determine the drop you require for the tablecloth and add 3 cm (1 ⅛ in) for the fringing allowance. Fringing works best on a rectangular or square tablecloth.

MATERIALS

Piece of fabric, 32 cm x 42 cm (12 ¾ in x 16 ¾ in) for each placemat

27 cm (10 ⅝ in) square of fabric for each napkin

Sufficient fabric for the tablecloth, cut to size

Scissors

Pin or needle

METHOD

1 Ensure that all the fabric edges are as straight as possible.

2 Using a pin or needle, pull out the threads down each long side and then each short side of each piece so that you make approximately 2 cm (¾ in) of fringing on each side. For the tablecloth, make the fringing 3 cm (1 ⅛ in) wide.

Satin-stitched Napery

Before you begin

Measure the size of your table and determine the drop you require, then add 2.5 cm (1 in) for the hem allowance.

MATERIALS

Piece of fabric, 32.5 cm x 42.5 cm (13 ¼ in x 17 in) for each placemat

32.5 cm (13 ¼ in) square of fabric for each napkin

Sufficient fabric for the tablecloth, cut to size

Machine or contrasting sewing machine thread

Sewing machine

Scissors

Tape measure

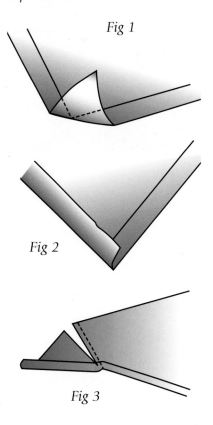

Fig 1

Fig 2

Fig 3

Primary brights in crisp cotton are the perfect choice for these satin stitched napkins and tablecloth.

METHOD

The method is the same for all items.

1 Turn in and press 2.5 cm (1 in) on all the raw edges, mitring the corner (Figs. 1 to 3 on previous page).

2 Machine stitch a satin stitch order around all sides over the raw edge. Remember to pivot at the corners.

Napkin with Contrast Border

MATERIALS

47 cm (18 ³⁄₈ in) square of fabric

Four strips of contrasting border fabric, each 8 cm x 47 cm

(3 in x 18 ³⁄₈ in) (you can vary the width to suit the fabric pattern)

1.8 m (2 yd) of purchased bias binding or 1.8 m (2 yd) of 3 cm (1 ¹⁄₈ in) wide bias-cut fabric strips

Matching sewing machine thread

Pins

Tape measure

Sewing machine

METHOD

1 Turn in and press 1 cm (³⁄₈ in) along the long inner edge of each border strip. Cut the ends to perfect diagonals, then join them with mitred corners.

2 Place the border strip and the fabric square together so that the right side of the

border faces the wrong side of the square. Stitch around the outside edge. Trim the corners, then turn the napkin to the right side and press.

3 Press the bias binding over double width the wrong sides together. Tuck the bias binding under the inner pressed edge of the border, leaving 5 mm (¹⁄₄ in) of the bias binding protruding. Stitch the inner pressed edge down into place, stitching through all thicknesses.

4 If you are using ribbon or braid which has finished edges, there is a very simple method you can use to achieve the same result. Turn in and press 1 cm (³⁄₈ in) on the edges of the napkin, then turn in and press another 1 cm (³⁄₈ in). Stitch. Pin the ribbon or braid around the edge of the napkin, folding the corners as shown (Figs. 1 to 3). Stitch down close to both edges of the ribbon or braid.

Placemat with Contrast Border

MATERIALS

Two pieces of main fabric, each 44 cm x 58 cm (17 ¹⁄₂ in x 23 in)

Piece of wadding, 44 cm x 58 cm (17 ¹⁄₂ in x 23 in)

Approximately 2.10 m (84 in) of contrasting fabric for the border

1.35 m (54 in) purchased bias binding or 3 cm (1 ¹⁄₈ in) wide bias-cut fabric strip in a contrasting colour

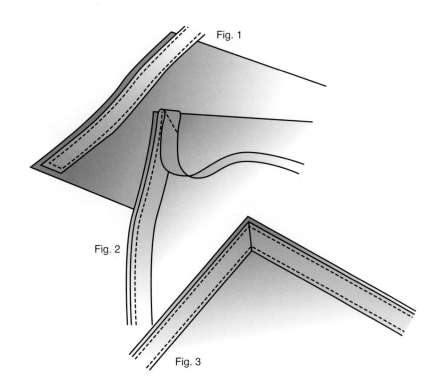

Fig. 1

Fig. 2

Fig. 3

Matching sewing machine thread
Pins
Scissors
Tape measure
Sewing machine

METHOD

1 Place the main fabric pieces with wrong sides facing and the wadding sandwiched between them. Baste. Quilt through all thicknesses in a pattern of your choice.

2 From the contrasting fabric, cut four strips, two 10 cm x 44 cm (4 in x 17 ½ in) and two 10 cm x 58 cm (4 in x 23 in). Turn in and press 1 cm (⅜ in) on the long inner edge of each strip. Cut the ends of the strips to perfect diagonals, then join them together with mitred corner (Fig. 1).

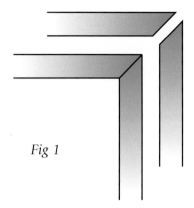

Fig 1

3 With right sides facing and the raw edges matching, stitch the border to the main piece. Trim the corners, then turn the placemat through to the right side and press.

4 Press the bias binding over double with the wrong sides together. Tuck the bias binding under the inner pressed edge of the border, leaving 5 mm of the bias binding protruding.

Stitch the inner pressed edge down into place, stitching through all thicknesses.

Napkin with contrast border, placemat with contrast border, appliquéd linen napkins.

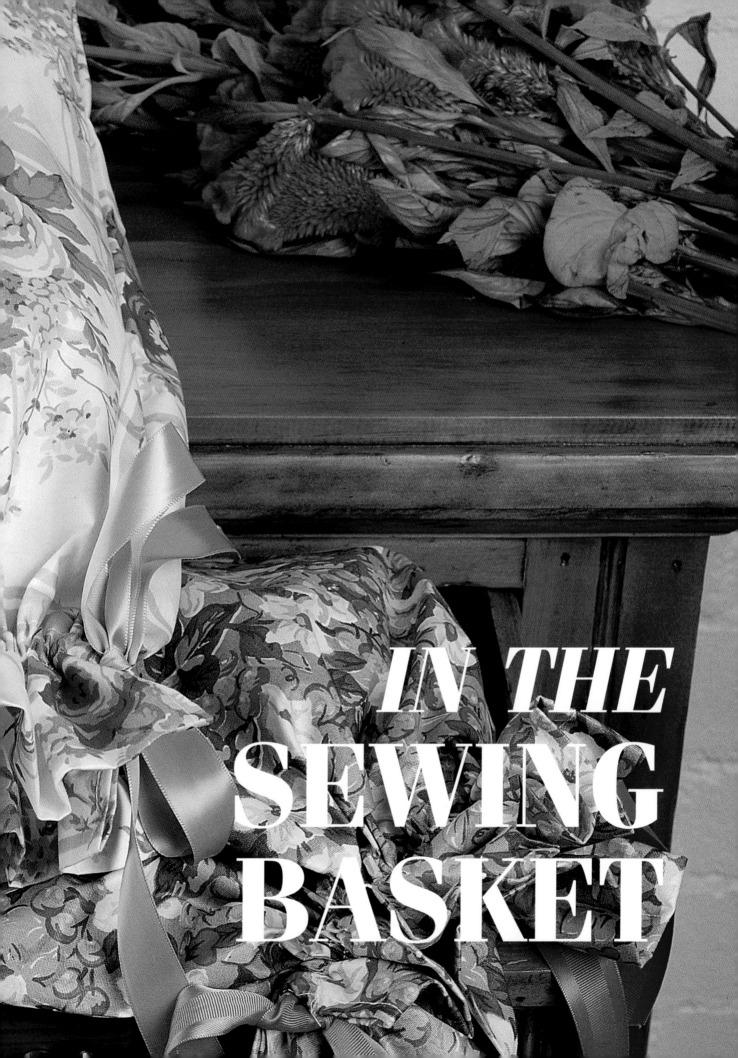

IN THE
SEWING
BASKET

Hussif

Traditionally a folding bag or roll taken by men going to war in 1914–18, the hussif is a useful way to keep all your sewing tools at hand.

   With a name that may be a corruption of 'housewife', the hussif was seen to replace the sewing and mending services usually performed by a housewife, with a pin cushion and compartments for thimble, tape measure, buttons and scissors. The original hussif was made in the form of a sleeve which kept all the equipment handy while leaving both hands free to work. Many of the original hussifs were very decorative.

MATERIALS

50 cm (20 in) of Liberty print fabric for the outer cover

50 cm (20 in) of plain lightweight fabric for the lining (it is best to use a natural fibre, not a synthetic one)

18 cm x 44 cm (7 ¼ in x 17 ½ in) of Pellon

Small amount of polyester fibrefill

50 cm (20 in) of lightweight iron-on Vilene

Small amount of flannel for the needlebook

Straw needle, largest size

Piecemakers crewel embroidery needles, sizes 8 or 9

Invisible press stud

Wooden beads or little buttons

Small piece of soft leather or chamois

Matching sewing thread

Fineline permanent marker pen

An assortment of coloured embroidery threads to complement the outer fabric including Perle No. 5 and a stranded cotton for button loops etc in the same colour

METHOD

See the patterns below.

Note: Compartments can be made from either the lining fabric or the Liberty.

1 Cut out the following pieces: the long hussif, 22 cm x 64 cm (8 ¾ in x 25 ⅜ in) from the Liberty fabric; the piece for quilting, 18 cm x 60 cm (7 ¼ in x 24 in) from the lining fabric and 18 cm x 20 cm (7 ¼ in x 8 in) from the Vilene; the button pocket, 10 cm x 37 cm (4 in x 14 ⅞ in) from the lining or the outer fabric.

2 Cut out the pattern pieces as indicated on the pattern sheet.

3 On the piece for quilting, place the Pellon on the back of the fabric piece. Baste them together, then quilt 44 cm (17 ½ in) of the length of the piece in a square grid.

4 On the sleeve, press the Vilene onto the middle of the fabric piece. Join the two short ends of the piece with a 1 cm (⅜ in) seam.

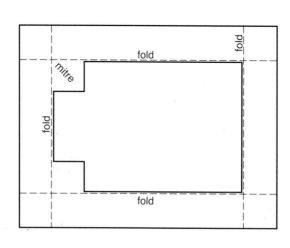

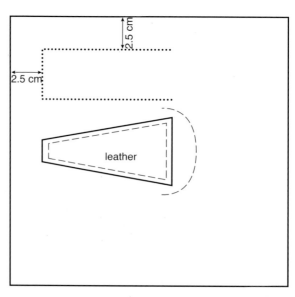

For the needlebook

For the outer fabric and lining section, press the Vilene onto the back of both pieces then place them together with the right sides facing and sew around the edge with a 5 mm (¼ in) seam, leaving a small opening for turning. Turn the piece to the right side and press carefully.

For the thimble pocket

Press the Vilene piece onto one end of the fabric piece. Fold the piece along the fold line with the right sides together. Sew around the edge with a 5 mm (¼ in) seam, leaving a small opening for turning. Turn the piece to the right side and press carefully.

For the scissors holder

Make the scissors holder in the same way as the thimble pocket.

For the button pocket

Fold the button pocket in half along the long side. Cut out a piece of Vilene, using the pattern provided. Press the

Vilene onto one half, placing the round end at the fold. Sew around the edge in the shape of the Vilene, leaving a small opening for turning. Trim the corners, turn and press.

For the tape pocket

Iron the tape pocket A piece of Vilene onto the middle of the fabric piece (Fig. 1). Fold in the fabric around the edge to the shape of the Vilene. Press well. Press tape pocket B piece of Vilene over the tape pocket A with the folds sandwiched in between. Press it in place. Mitre the two corners at one end, stitching the mitres into place with small slipstitches.

For the pin cushion

1 Iron the Vilene onto the backs of the fabric pieces. Sew them together with a 5 mm (¼ in) seam, with the right sides facing and leaving a small opening. Turn and press. Stuff the pin cushion with the fibrefill, then close the opening.

Note: Now you must decide which side will be the top of your pincushion. Take into account where you will place your embroidery and how much you are planning to do.

2 Thread the straw needle with a 160 cm (64 in) length of the Perle No. 5 thread and knot one end. Measure across the diameter of the pin cushion at two angles and mark the point where these lines intersect (the centre) with a pin. Do the same on the other side. Pass the needle through the centre of the top of the pin cushion, pulling hard to take the knot into the stuffing. Take the needle through to the centre of the bottom. Pulling the thread very, very firmly, divide the pin cushion into half, then quarters, then eighths by wrapping the thread around and passing it back through the centre. It is important that you pull the thread hard in order to create the pumpkin-like shape. When you have made the last wrap, finishing at the bottom of the pin cushion, make a small buttonhole stitch bar across the threads, then finish off by passing the thread back through the pin cushion.

EMBROIDERY

1 Using double knot stitch, the straw needle and the Perle No. 5 thread, embroider around the needlebook, the scissors holder and the thimble pocket. Fold the button pocket. Fold the button pocket and the thimble pocket into small bag

shapes, then work along the sides in double knot stitch to join them. Work around the pin cushion in double knot stitch, taking care to slip the needle under the binding to keep the pumpkin shape.

2 Using two strands of cotton, work double feather stitch across the two short ends of the sleeve.

3 A third of the way down the back of the thimble pocket, work a small buttonhole stitch bar. Work two small buttonhole stitch bars on the back of the button pocket. Work around the Vilene-backed flannel pieces with buttonhole stitch.

4 Embellish the compartments with your choice of embroidery. Taking your inspiration from the outer fabric always gives a pretty effect.

FINISHING

1 Press the sleeve piece flat with the seam at the centre back. Measure down 2.54 cm (1 in) from the top and left side. Using the marker pen, mark these lines with small dots (Fig. 2). Using a basting stitch sew the tape pocket in place, between the dotted lines.

2 Trim the leather or chamois to the shape of the scissors holder. Hand-sew one half to the back of the scissors holder, then fold the leather in half. Position the scissors holder on the sleeve, then sew the free half of the leather or chamois to the sleeve. Sew the scissors holder to the sleeve.

3 Attach the button pocket, thimble pocket and pin cushion to the sleeve by sewing through the bar on the back.

4 Make a 10 cm (4 in) cord from the remaining Perle No. 5 thread. Fold over one end to make a small slug and stitch to secure. Sew this to the top of the invisible press stud. Sew the other end of the cord through the sleeve. This little cord is for holding the scissors in place.

5 Place the long hussif and the quilted piece together with the wrong sides facing. Roll in the sides of the long hussif to cover the edges of the quilted piece and baste them in place. Measure down 15 cm (6 in) and open the stitching to fit the sleeve into place, then rebaste.

6 Starting at the top right-hand corner, using the crewel needle and two strands of cotton, work double feather stitch all around, securing the rolled edge and the sleeve as you go. Remove the basting.

7 At the bottom edge, fold up 11.5 cm (4 ½ in) forming a pocket. Sew the sides with double knot stitch.

8 Sew the flannel pieces to the needlebook, then attach the needlebook over the quilted piece.

9 Cover two wooden beads with the remaining Perle No. 5. Make buttonhole stitch bars at the top of the hussif. Roll up to position the beads, then sew on the beads.

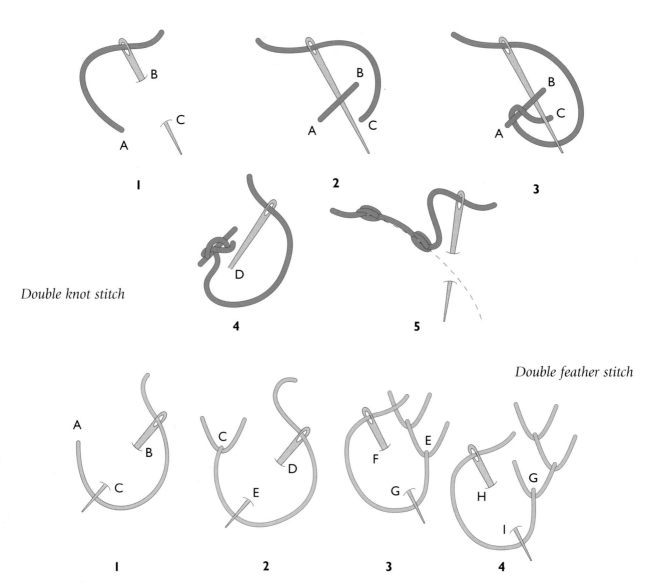

Double knot stitch

Double feather stitch

STITCH GUIDE

Double knot stitch

Pull the thread through from the back at A. Insert the needle at B, bringing it up again at C. Pull the thread through (Fig. 1).

Without piercing the fabric, run the needle under the stitch and pull the thread through (Fig. 2).

Make a loop as shown and again run the needle under the stitch at B and over the thread at C. Pull the thread through (Fig. 3).

For a single stitch, take the needle to the back of the work at D (Fig. 4). For a sequence, carry the thread to the position of the next stitch and repeat (Fig. 5).

Double feather stitch

Pull the thread through from the fabric at A inserting it at B and making a loop as shown. Bring the needle out at C, keeping the thread beneath the needle. Pull the thread through (Fig. 1).

Insert the needle at D bringing it out again at E, making a loop as shown. Again, keep the thread under the needle (Fig. 2).

Insert the needle at F, bringing it out at G and making a loop as before (Fig 3).

Insert the needle at H, bringing it out at I and making a loop as before (Fig 4). Continue working in this way, placing two stitches to the right and two stitches to the left. Secure the last stitch with a small stitch over the loop.

Drawstring Bag

A drawstring bag can be used for many decorative yet practical applications.

BEFORE YOU BEGIN
Choose a fabric appropriate for the proposed use of the bag; PVC fabric could be used for toiletries, and a light sheer fabric could be used for lingerie. A brightly coloured children's print could be used to take toys to grandma's, or used as a library or book bag, or even for carrying a sleeping sheet to kindergarten. You can make the bag any size you like; the measurements given here are for a toiletry bag.

MATERIALS

60 cm (24 in) fabric

1.6 m (64 in) drawstring cord or ribbon

Matching sewing machine thread

Tailor's chalk

Sewing machine

METHOD

1 Fold the fabric over double, lengthways, with the right sides together. Stitch the sides together in a 1.5 cm (⅝ in) seam. Neaten the raw edges with overlocking or zigzag stitching.

2 Turn the bag through to the right side. Turn in and press 5 mm (¼ in) at the top edge then turn in and press another 5 cm (2 in). Stitch through all thicknesses along the fold and again 1.5 cm (⅝ in) away, forming a casing.

3 Open the stitching at the side seams for approximately 1.5 cm (⅝ in). Thread an 80 cm (32 in) length of cord or ribbon in one opening through the whole casing and out the same opening. Repeat for the other 80 cm (32 in) of cord or ribbon, threading it through the other opening. Knot the ends of the cord or ribbon together.

Scented Shoe Stuffers

MATERIALS

20 cm (8 in) of 115 cm (45 in) wide cotton fabric

Polyester stuffing, lavender or potpourri

Lace and ribbon for trimming

METHOD

1 Cut four shapes from fabric. With right sides facing and raw edges even, stitch pairs together around curved edge. Clip seams. Turn and press.

2 Turn under 4 mm (³⁄₁₆ in) at raw edge and again at 6 mm (¼ in). Stitch. Trim with lace if desired.

3 Fill shoe stuffers as desired. Tie bows made from ribbon or self-fabric bias around tops to secure.

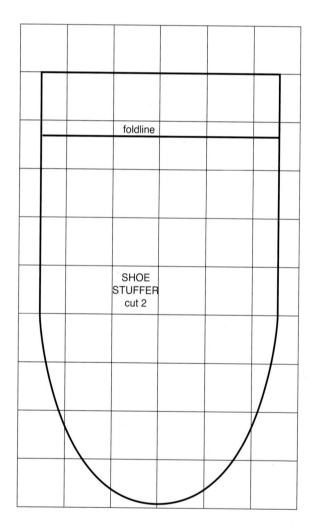

foldline

SHOE STUFFER cut 2

EMBROIDERY

Afghan

Simplicity itself, this versatile afghan combines beauty and practicality. Throw it over the back of a chair for instant decoration.

MATERIALS

125 cm (50 in) panel of Anne cloth (this will give you 6 squares x 9 squares)

Tapestry needle, size 24

DMC Stranded Cotton: Green 935, Dark Red 315

EMBROIDERY

See the embroidery graphs on page 91.

Note: There are six cross stitch designs in the afghan (Figs 1–6). Embroider them in the colour indicated in the position shown in the placement diagram. The designs are stitched over two

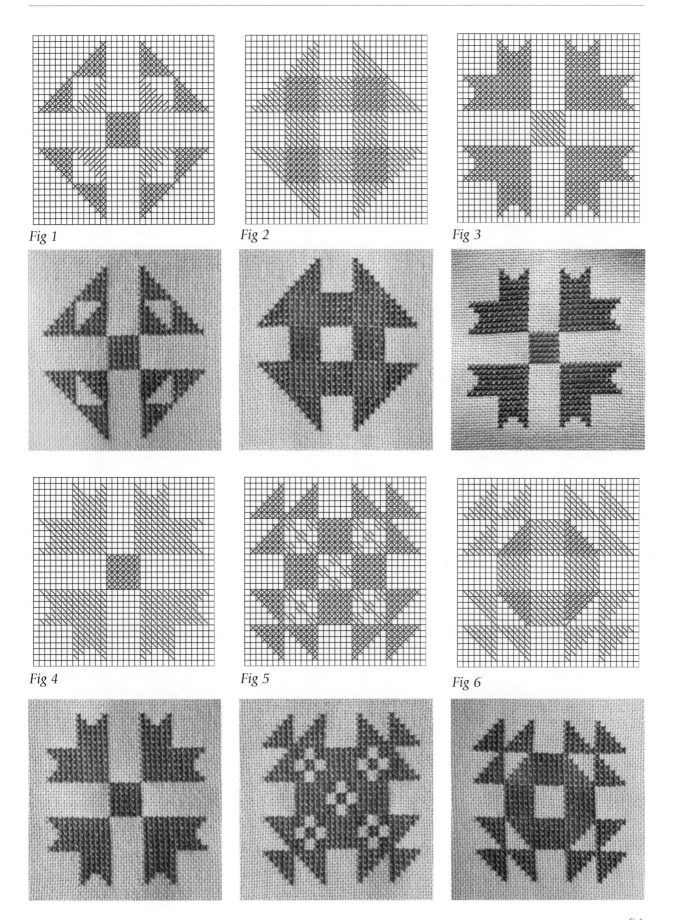

Fig 1

Fig 2

Fig 3

Fig 4

Fig 5

Fig 6

threads of the Anne cloth, using three strands of the cotton. Because the work can be seen on the back, try to make all the stitches on the back horizontal and as neat as possible. Once the embroidery is completed, press the work on the wrong side.

Trim the afghan to 5 cm (2 in) bigger than the six quare by nine square finished size. Make the fringed border by drawing threads for a depth of 5 cm (2 in) on all sides. Tie each group of eight threads into a knot at the base.

Draught Stoppers

These may not keep the wolf from the door, but they will surely keep out the chill.

MATERIALS

Strip of velvet 22 cm x 115 cm (8 ¾ in x 45 in)

Embroidery thread for grub roses

Strong ribbon or braid for tying ends

Clean sand for filling

METHOD

1 Embroider an oval of grub roses onto centre of velvet and 25 cm (10 in) from each end, following instruction in *How to embroider grub roses* (as shown).

2 Fold velvet so that long sides are even and right sides are facing. Stitch long side in 1 cm (⅜ in) seam. Turn.

3 Fold in 10 cm (4 in) at one end. Tie off very securely about 8 cm (3 in) from end. Fill with sand, using a funnel. Shake frequently to settle sand. When tube is filled fold in 10 cm (4 in) at open end and tie off securely as before.

How to embroider grub roses

Grub roses are stitched in toning shades of stranded cotton, starting with darkest shade at centre and working out to lightest shade. Stitch leaves in bullion knots or chain stitch in tones of green. Bring needle up at A. Take a stitch from B to A; do not pull needle through (A to B equals the width of knot required). Twist thread several times around needle clockwise covering width of AB. Pull needle through easing twisted thread onto fabric. Re-insert needle at B. Build up bullion knots as shown.

Embroidered Pin Cushion

This beautiful combination of dupion silk, wonderful lace and silk ribbon embroidery makes a very stylish accessory.

MATERIALS

Sudsberry House Shaker box pin cushion

12 cm x 18 cm (4 ¾ in x 7 ¼ in) of bottle green dupion silk

18 cm (7 ¼ in) of 2 cm (¾ in) wide needlerun insertion lace

1.5 m (1 ⅔ yd) of 4 mm (³⁄₁₆ in) wide silk ribbon, Deep Pink

1 m (40 in) each of 4 mm (³⁄₁₆ in) wide silk ribbon: Burgundy, Deep Green, Blue, Yellow

Piecemakers tapestry needle, size 24

Piecemakers crewel needle, size 9

Ordinary sewing thread, Cream

DMC Perle Cotton, No. 5, Burgundy

Embroidery hoop

450 craft glue

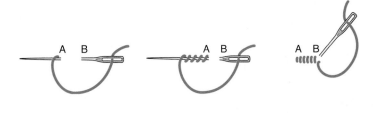

Fly stitch rose

METHOD

See the embroidery design and stitch guide on this page.

1 Using the Cream sewing thread, stitch the lace down the centre of the dupion silk.

2 Embroider the flowers over the lace, following the embroidery design and stitch guide.

3 When the embroidery is completed, make up the pin cushion, following the instructions supplied with the kit. Make sure the fabric sits quite smoothly all around the edges and it is glued firmly into the base.

TWISTED CORD

1 Cut four lengths of Perle cotton, each 2 m (2 yd 8 in) long. Tie them together with a knot at one end and secure this end to a chair back, door knob or something similar.

2 Holding the other end, twist the cord clockwise until it is so tight that it will twist against itself. You can test this as you go.

3 Fold the cord in half, allowing it to twist evenly. Cut the end that is secured to the chair or door and knot all the ends together.

4 Glue the twisted cord neatly around the pin cushion, tucking the ends under.

STITCH GUIDE

Fly stitch rose

Using the Deep Pink or the Burgundy silk ribbon, begin with a fly stitch, then add two more spokes. Build up the rose by weaving the ribbon tightly three times around the spokes, clockwise, then another two times loosely.

Daisy

Using Yellow silk ribbon, work five lazy daisy stitches. Work a Burgundy French knot for the centre.

Forget-me-not

Work six Blue French knots around a Yellow French knot centre.

Rose bud

Work a ribbon stitch bud to match the rose. For the stem and fly stitch, use a length of silk thread from the edge of the fabric.

Leaf

Work detached chain stitches in Deep Green.

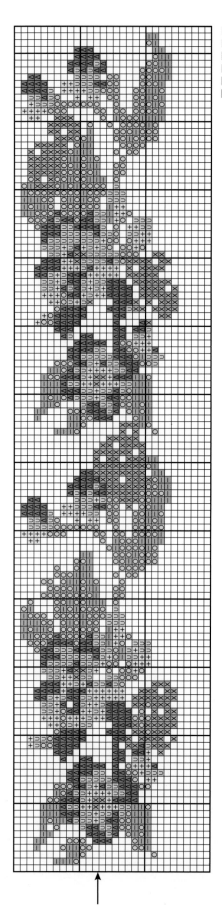

+ Light pink 48
U Medium pink 50
X Dark pink 62
O Light green 264
– Medium green 266
▲ Dark green 268

Fruit and Flower Border Designs (Cross Stitch)

Inspired by the beauty and bounty of the garden, these exquisite border designs can be used to embellish just about anything. Try stitching them on towels and bed-linens, around the lids of hatboxes, or onto tablecloths or placemats.

Don't limit yourself to combining these borders only with solid colours. Try edging pretty little cottage prints, or dainty pastel stripes and checks. Some of the designs are suitable to stitch as single motifs as well.

FINISHED SIZE
Each border is stitched on a 5 cm (2 in) wide band.

MATERIALS
5 cm (2 in) wide white 14-count Aida band in the desired length

Anchor Stranded Cotton in the colours listed in the Colour Keys; the number of skeins will depend on the number of repeats

Tapestry needle

PREPARATION
Mark the lengthwise centre of one end of the Aida band, about 5 cm (2 in) from the end.

U Orange 314
O Light purple 108
X Medium purple 111
+ Light green 278
— Medium green 280
△ Dark green 924

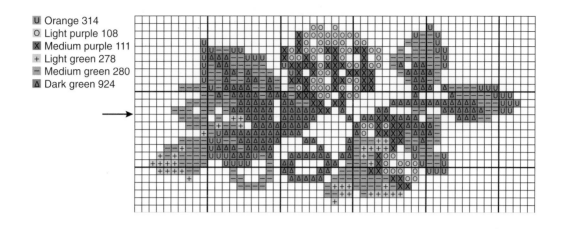

O Pink 63
◈ Crimson 65
+ Light purple 96
— Medium purple 99
△ Dark purple 101
U Light green 225
X Medium green 228

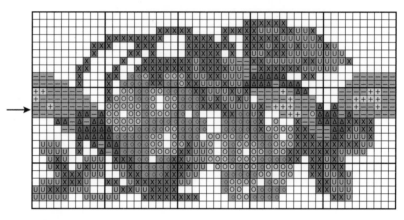

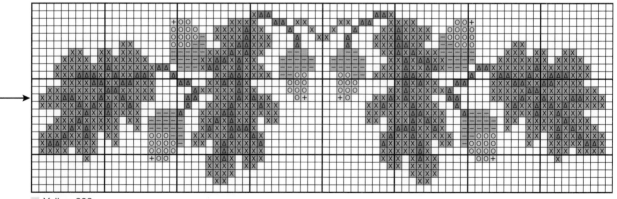

+ Yellow 293
○ Light dusty pink 893
— Medium dusty pink 895
X Olive 844
△ Dark green 924

CROSS STITCH

Following the Chart and with three strands of cotton, cross stitch the design onto the Aida band, beginning the stitching by matching the centre of the band with the arrow on the Chart. Continue repeating the design motif for the length required. Leave ten rows between each purple flower motif, three between the oak and acorn motifs, and five between the pink flower motifs. The remaining borders are continuous.

FINISHING

Press the completed cross stitch face down on a padded surface.

Hot-water Bottle Cover

Snuggle into bed on a cold evening with your hot-water bottle tucked into this pretty cover and you're sure to stay cosy all night.

MATERIALS

28 cm x 80 cm (11 in x 32 in) of wool blanketing

DMC Tapestry Wool, one skein each: Blue/black 7339; Pink 7132, 7151, 7202, 7204, 7211, 7251; Green 7333, 7376, 7377, 7386, 7424, 7426; Orange 7124; Yellow 7503, 7504, 7579; Blue 7314, 7593, 7797, 7799; Ecru; Violet 7241, 7262, 7266, 7268; Brown 7419; Beige 7521

28 cm x 80 cm (11 in x 32 in) of lining fabric

Doll-making needle

Assorted tapestry needles

Blue water-soluble marker pen

Ordinary sewing cotton to match the wool blanketing

80 cm (32 in) of cord or ribbon

Note: For wool embroidery, use a needle which the wool will comfortably fit through without causing wear to the strand. Occasionally, move the position of the thread in relation to the needle so the stress is not concentrated at the same point. This will also reduce fraying.

Because wool will not fit through the eye of a straw needle, a doll-making needle is used to make an even wrap on the bullion stitch. The doll-making needle is similar to a straw or milliner's needle in that its body and shaft are the same width, making it easier to pull the wraps through evenly.

All the wools used here are tapestry wools, but some have been stranded. Use four strands throughout, unless otherwise instructed.

PREPARATION

See the embroidery design on page 101.

1 Fold the wool blanketing in half. Mark the fold with a line of basting. All the embroidery will be positioned on one side (front) of this line.

2 Photocopy the design, and cut out each separate item you are going to stitch, then trace around it on the front of the blanketing, using the blue marker pen.

EMBROIDERY

1 For the birdhouse, stem stitch the outline in Ecru, then fill in the house in stem stitch, starting from the top and working down until the entire area has been filled. Straight stitch the roof in 7339 until the entire area has been filled in. Stem stitch the platform and the pole in two rows of stem stitch in 7339.

2 Stem stitch the gate in 7419, filling the entire shape with stem stitches.

3 Stem stitch the path in 7521, creating a crazy-paving pattern.

4 For the roses over the gate, the centre is stitched in bullion stitch in two strands of 7504. The outside wrap is stitched in bullion stitch in two strands of 7579. Stitch the leaves in lazy daisy stitch in two strands of 7426. The stem is stitched in 7419 stem stitch.

5 Stitch the buds on the topiary tree in fly stitch with two strands of 7333 around the buds, stitched in two strands of Ecru. In the centre, work a fly stitch in two strands of 7204. Stitch the foliage on the topiary tree in bullion stitch in two strands of 7333.

6 For the roses on the topiary tree, start from the centre with three straight stitches in two strands of 7202. For the next round, work a series of straight stitches, following the circle around in two strands of 7132. For the last round, work in straight stitch in two strands of Ecru in the same way. Stitch the stem in two stem stitch rows of 7333.

7 Stitch the shaded areas of the hollyhocks in blanket stitch in 7151 and the rest in blanket stitch in 7211. The leaves are stitched in small lazy daisy stitch in 7377.

8 Stitch the red hot pokers in a series of bullion stitches in 7124 to form the flower heads. Work the stems in stem stitch in 7426.

9 Stitch the yellow daisy petals in lazy daisy stitch in 7503. Work French knots in the centre in two strands on 7799.

10 Stitch the cream daisy petals in bullion stitch, using two strands of Ecru. Stitch the centre in French knots in two strands of 7503.

11 Stitch massed French knots along the path, some in Ecru, some in 7262 and some in 7266. The stems are stitched in straight stitch in 7376.

12 Stitch the yellow part of the daffodils in 7503 in a series of straight stitches coming to a point at the centre and becoming smaller at the edges. The flower centre is worked in straight stitches in 7124. The stems are stitched in stem stitch in 7426. Work two rows of stem stitch in the same colour for the leaves.

13 The blue flowers are worked in a series of French knots in three strands that are worked in a straight line. The darker colour 7797 at the bottom, next 7593, the 7799 at the top.

14 Stitch the stems of the small orange flowers in stem stitch in two strands of 7376. The flowers are stitched in straight stitch in two strands of 7124.

15 For the forget-me-nots, work the centres in 7503 French knots. The petals are stitched in French knots in 7799.

16 Stitch the pink flowers in lazy daisy stitch in 7521. The foliage is worked in lazy daisy stitch in 7424.

17 Stitch the foliage of the irises in two rows of stem stitch in 7386, and the stems in one row of the same colour. Stitch the flowers in lazy daisy stitch, placing 7268 on the outside, 7241 on the inside and a French knot in 7503 in the centre.

18 For the purple flowers on the right side of the path, stitch a series of French knots in 7262, with the leaves in lazy daisy stitch in 7376.

19 Stitch the lighter bluebells in buttonhole stitch in 7799. Stitch the darker flowers in buttonhole stitch in 7314 and the leaves in stem stitch in 7426.

20 Stitch the bird in satin stitch in Ecru. Stitch the beak in straight stitch in one strand of 7124. Stitch a French knot for the eye in one strand of 7799.

MAKING UP

1 Stitch two buttonhole stitches by hand in the front of the hot-water bottle cover, approximately 7 cm (2 ¾ in) from the top of the cover.

2 Sew the side seams of the embroidered piece and of the lining. Turn the embroidered piece right side out. Place the lining inside the embroidered piece so the wrong sides are facing.

3 Turn down 2.54 cm (1 in) on the raw edge of the embroidered piece and 3.5 cm (1 ⅜ in) on the raw edge of the lining. Slipstitch the folded edge of the lining to the embroidered piece.

4 Using the ordinary sewing cotton, stitch a casing for the cord or ribbon. Thread the cord or ribbon through the casing.

Nordic Border Designs

Rich blue contrasting with vivid white is often used for embroidery in northern Europe. Inspired by the homes, children and the folk art of the region, these borders can be used to embellish a variety of home accessories.

The house picture would be beautiful framed as a single motif, as well as repeated for a border. Try using any of the three elements from the folk border as separate borders, or stitch the children as single motifs.

FINISHED SIZE

The house border is 11.5 cm x 33 cm (4 ½ in x 13 ¼ in); the folk border is 11.5 cm (4 ½ in) wide.

MATERIALS

White 14-count Aida cloth in the desired size

Anchor Stranded Cotton in the colours listed in the Colour Keys; the number of skeins will depend on the number of repeats

Tapestry needle

PREPARATION

Cut the fabric larger than the desired size. Finish the edges of the fabric to prevent fraying. Mark the centres of the Chart and of the fabric.

Cross stitch

Following the Chart and the Colour Key, cross stitch the designs onto the fabric using three strands of cotton, beginning the stitching at the centre. For the folk border leave two horizontal fabric rows between each repeat. Continue repeating the design motifs on either side of the centre for the length required. With two strands of Blue, back stitch following the Chart.

FINISHING

Press the completed cross stitch face down on a padded surface.

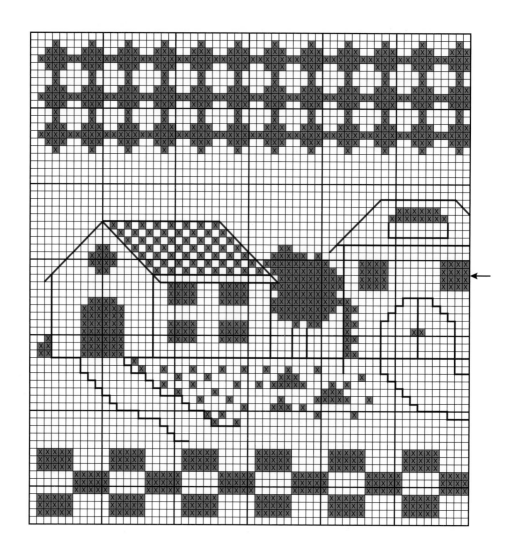

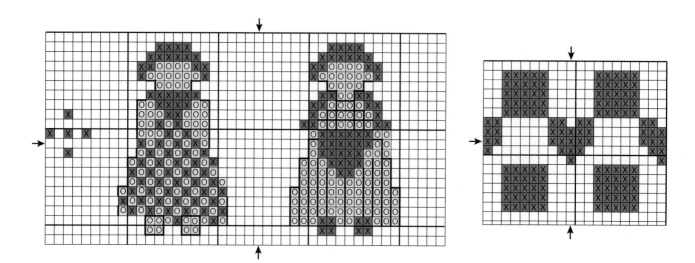

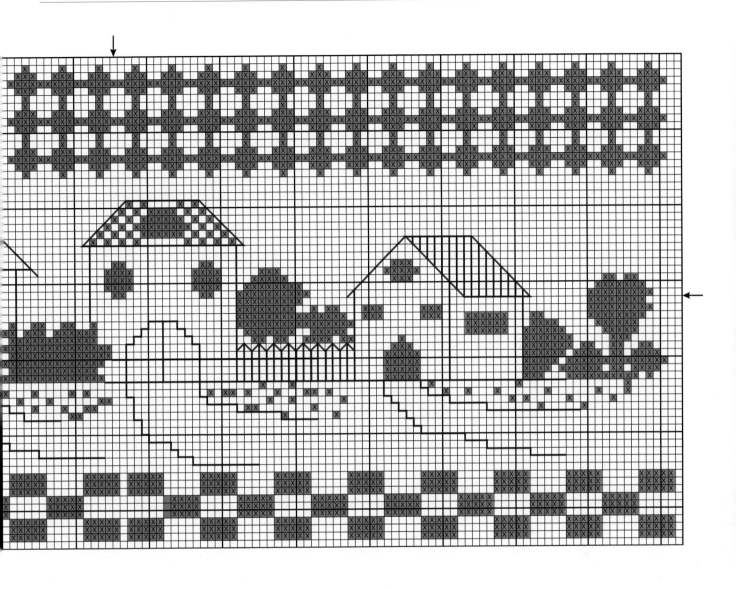

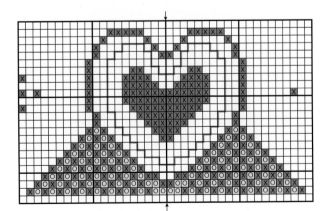

Sacred Cross

Ecclesiastical embroidery has a wonderful history. This piece is an unusual variation on the traditional techniques as it uses tiny roses to define the cross.

MATERIALS

30 cm (12 in) square of antique gold dupion silk

Crewel needle, size 10

Straw needle, size 10

Madeira Silk Embroidery Floss, Black

Madeira Metallic Embroidery Thread, Gold

Stranded cotton:

DMC	MADEIRA
315	0810
902	0601
3052	1509
3041	0806
781	2213
Ecru	Ecru
932	1710

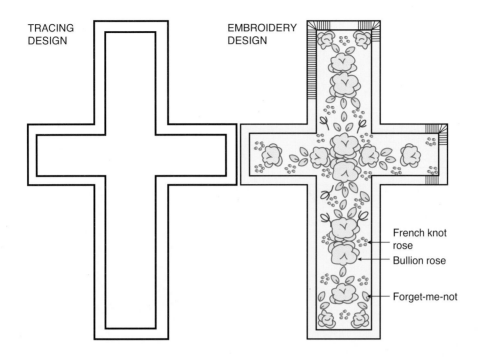

TRACING DESIGN

EMBROIDERY DESIGN

French knot rose

Bullion rose

Forget-me-not

Note: This piece has been stitched in Madeira Stranded Cotton.

PREPARATION

See the tracing and the embroidery design on this page.

Trace the outline of the cross onto the centre of the fabric.

Embroidery

Note: Embroider the flowers following the Embroidery Guide above and the stitch guide on page 206. All the embroidery is worked in one strand unless stated otherwise.

1 Using the crewel needle, commence embroidering around the outer edge of the cross, using the Black silk thread and back stitch. Work around inner and outer edges of border in this way. When the outline is completed, fill in the border with satin stitches in Black silk thread.

2 Using the straw needle, embroider the main roses and leaves first. For the bullion roses, begin with a bullion stitch approximately 4 mm (³/₁₆ in) long for the centre of the rose. Work the centres in 0601, the petals in 0810 and the leaves in 1509.

3 Using the straw needle, embroider the Ecru single roses in French knots of three twists around the needle. Work a French knot of two twists around the needle in Black silk for the centre.

4 Using the straw needle, embroider forget-me-nots in French knots in 1710 through the design, then add more French knots in 0806 and 0810. Work French knots in the centres of the forget-me-nots in 2213. All these French knots have two twists around the needle. Keep filling in with French knots until there are no bare spots.

5 Using the crewel needle and one strand of metallic thread, outline the outer and inner edge of the border in back stitch.

6 Trim the embroidery to the shape and size you prefer, the rectangle shape shown here complements the shape of the cross very well.

Scarecrow Blanket

With its rich red colour and charmingly simple embroidery, this blanket is great fun.

MATERIALS

80 cm x 115 cm (32 in x 45 in) of blanket wool

1.5 m (1 ⅔ yd) of backing fabric

10 cm (4 in) square of plaid fabric for the overalls

4.1 m (4 ½ yd) of piping cord

Piecemaker tapestry needles, size 22

Appleton's Crewel Wool: Dark Brown, Yellow, Green, Blue, Green, Jade or Navy Blue, Pale Green, Pale Yellow, Tan, Light Brown, Burgundy

Matching sewing thread

METHOD

See the Embroidery Design and the Overalls Pattern on page 109.

109

1 Measure 40 cm (16 in) up from one end of the blanket and baste a line across the blanket at this point. This will be the base line of the embroidery.

2 Using the pattern, cut out a pair of overalls from the plaid fabric. Baste the overalls into position, then hand-appliqué, turning under a small seam allowance with the tip of the needle as you go.

3 Embroider the flowers and the rest of the scarecrow, following the embroidery design on page 109 and the stitch guide on this page.

ASSEMBLING

1 Cut four lengths across the width of the backing fabric, each 2.5 cm (1 in) wide. Fold them over double with the wrong sides together and the raw edges even. Place lengths of piping cord inside and, using the zipper foot on your sewing machine, stitch close to the piping cord.

2 Lay the backing fabric face down. Centre the embroidered wool, face upwards, on the backing so there is a 10 cm (4 in) border of backing visible all around. If necessary, trim the backing to achieve this. Baste from the centre out to the edges and to the corners, and around all the edges.

3 Pin the piping to the blanket, 5 cm (2 in) from the edge, with the cord facing the centre of the blanket.

 Fold the backing fabric to meet the blanket edge, then fold it again to meet the piping cord. Pin the border into place,

mitring the corners. Slipstitch through the fabric, piping and blanket, but not through the backing. Remove all the basting.

STITCH GUIDE

Sunflower

The centre is made up of massed French knots in Dark Brown.

The petals are Yellow lazy daisy stitches — as many as are needed to surround the centre.

For the leaves, begin with a straight stitch, then work as many open fly stitches in Green as are needed to arrive at the correct size.

The stem is one long straight stitch in Green, couched down with small stitches every 1 cm (⅜ in).

Dandelion

For the seed head, work open fly stitches into the centre in Pale Yellow.

The stem is one straight stitch in Pale Green.

The leaves are four lazy daisy stitches in Pale Green, two small ones, then two larger ones.

Forget-me-not

Each petal is made up of three Blue straight stitches worked on top of each other. Work a Yellow French knot in the centre of five petals.

The leaves are small lazy daisy stitches in Green.

Pumpkin

The pumpkin is worked in Tan stem stitches with a Brown straight stitch stalk.

Scarecrow

The boots (Brown), sticks (Brown), shirt outline (Jade or Navy Blue) and hat (Tan) are all stem stitch. The shirt is completed with couched lines of straight stitch.

The hair is straight stitch worked in two strands of Yellow.

The eyes are cross stitches in Yellow.

Bird

The bird's body is worked in Burgundy stem stitch and the feathers are lazy daisy stitches in the same colour.

Seashell Pillows

These beautiful pillows will remind you wistfully of those late afternoon strolls along the beach collecting shells, driftwood, starfish and feathers. Blue and white fabric adds a feeling of summer freshness.

FINISHED SIZE

The pillows are 36 cm (14 ½ in) square, plus edgings. The shells and starfish stitched design is 22.5 cm (8 ⅞ in) square. The blue shells stitch design is 21 cm x 30 cm (8 ⅜ in x 12 in).

MATERIALS

Shells and starfish pillow

36 cm (14 ½ in) square of white 14-count Aida cloth

One skein each of Anchor Stranded Cotton in the colours listed in the Colour Key, or the number of skeins shown in parentheses

70 cm (28 in) of cotton plaid fabric

36 cm (14 ½ in) square pillow form

Small amount of wadding

Tapestry needle

Matching sewing thread

Blue shells pillow

38 cm (15 in) square of white 14-count Aida cloth

One skein each of Anchor Stranded Cotton in the colours listed in the Colour Key or the number of skeins shown in parentheses

70 cm (28 in) of cotton print fabric

36 cm (14 ½ in) square pillow form

Small amount of wadding

Tapestry needle

Matching sewing thread

PREPARATION

Finish the edges of the Aida fabric to prevent fraying. Mark the centres of the Chart and of the fabric.

Cross stitch

Following the Chart and Colour Key, cross stitch the design onto the fabric using three strands of cotton, beginning the stitching at the centre.

FINISHING

Shells and starfish pillow

1 Press the complete cross stitch face down on a padded surface. Trim the Aida to 33 cm (13 ¼ in) square.

2 From the plaid fabric, cut 15 cm (6 in) wide strips and sew them to the top and bottom of the cross stitched piece. Sew two strips to the side edges with a 12 mm (½ in) seam to make the pillow front. Mitre the corners. Cut the back the same size as the front.

3 Place the front and back with the right sides together and the raw edges matching. Stitch them together with a 12 mm (½ in) seam, leaving an opening in the centre of one side. Turn the pillow cover right side out. Cut 2.5 cm (1 in) wide strips of wadding. Place them inside the edges of the pillow cover. Insert the pillow form and slipstitch the opening closed. Stitch a row 2.5 cm (1 in) in from all edges.

Blue shells pillow

1 Press the completed cross stitch face down on a padded surface.

2 From the print fabric cut two strips 5 cm x 38 cm (2 in x 15 in) for the front sides. Stitch the side pieces to the front piece to complete. Cut the back the same size. Cut two strips 18 cm (7 ¼ in) x the width of the fabric for the ruffle.

3 Stitch the shorter ends of the ruffle strips together to form a loop. Press the strip in half with the wrong sides together. Divide the loop into four quarters and mark each quarter. Stitch two rows of gathering stitches along the raw edges, and gather the strip up to fit the pillow front, matching the marked quarters with the corners. Baste the ruffle in place.

4 Place the front and back with the right sides together and the raw edges matching, and stitch them together with a 12 mm (½ in) seam, leaving an opening in the centre of one side. Insert the pillow form and slipstitch the opening closed.

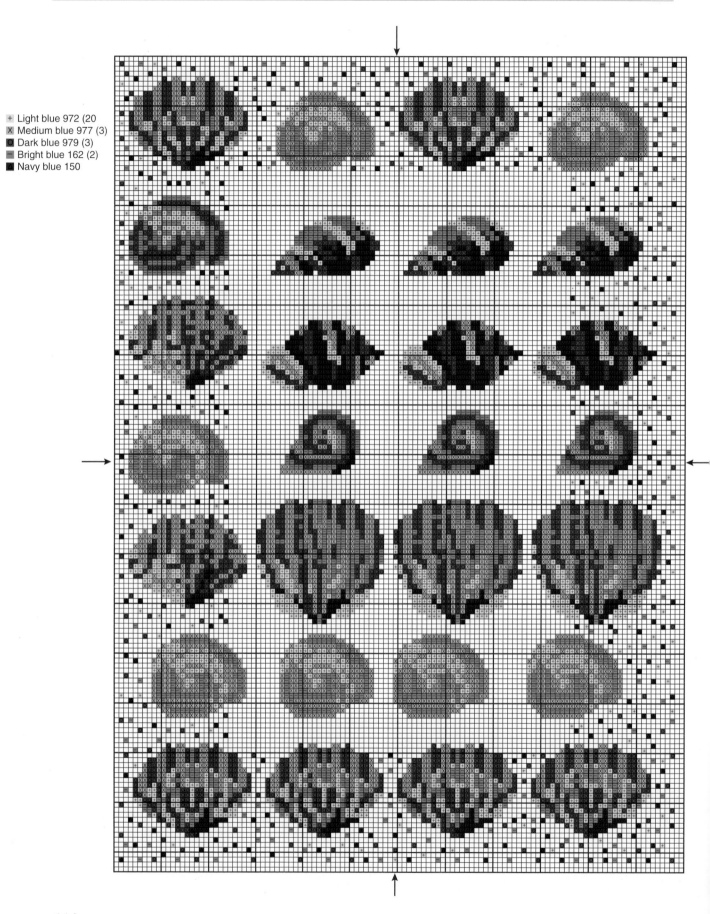

+ Light blue 972 (20
X Medium blue 977 (3)
◙ Dark blue 979 (3)
═ Bright blue 162 (2)
▲ Navy blue 150

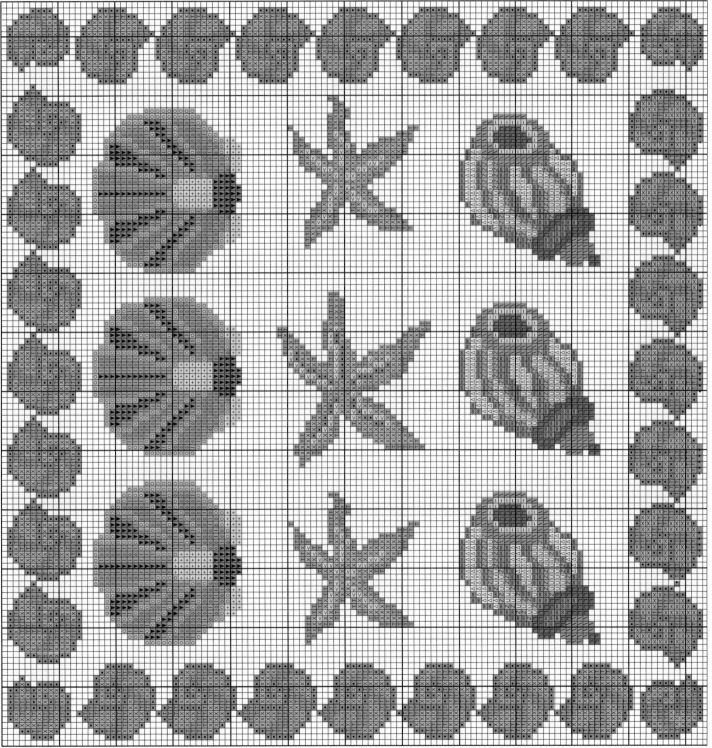

Silk Lavender Sachets

Be ready for the gift-giving season with these delightful embroidered sachets. They feature silk ribbon flowers that will delight you.

MATERIALS

For all four sachets

15 cm x 76 cm (6 in x 30 ⅜ in) of dupion silk

1 m (40 in) of ribbon

Small embroidery hoop

Lavender

For the pansy sachet

1 m (40 in) each of four colours of 7 mm (¼ in) wide silk ribbon (overdyed ribbons are very suitable)

2 m (80 in) of 4 mm (³⁄₁₆ in) wide silk ribbon, Dark Green

2 m (80 in) of 4 mm (³⁄₁₆ in) wide overdyed silk ribbon, Pale Pink

1 m (40 in) of 4 mm (³⁄₁₆ in) wide ribbon, Black or dark contrasting colour

1 m (40 in) of 4 mm (³⁄₁₆ in) wide silk ribbon, Yellow for the centres

DMC Stranded Cotton, Dark Green

Piecemaker tapestry needle, size 22

Piecemaker crewel needle, size 9

1 m (40 in) of 5 cm (2 in) wide French organza ribbon

For the rose bowl

10 m (11 yd 4 in) each of 4 mm (³⁄₁₆ in) wide ribbon: overdyed Pink/Lemon, Pink silk ribbon, Pale Pink silk ribbon

4.1 m (4 ½ yd) of 4 mm (³⁄₁₆ in) wide silk ribbon, Peach

8 m (9 yd) of 2 mm (¹⁄₁₆ in) wide silk ribbon, White

8 m (9 yd) of 4 mm (³⁄₁₆ in) wide silk ribbon, Beige/Green

DMC Stranded Cotton: Pale Green, Light Tan

Piecemaker tapestry needle, size 22

Piecemaker crewel needle, size 9

75 cm (30 in) each of two 5 cm (2 in) wide French organza ribbon

For the Canterbury bells

5 m (5 yd 20 in) each of 4 mm (³⁄₁₆ in) wide silk ribbon: two shades of Cream, four shades of Mauve

1 m (40 in) of 4 mm (³⁄₁₆ in) wide silk ribbon: Plum, Green

DMC Stranded Cotton, Dark Green

Piecemaker tapestry needle, size 22

Piecemaker crewel needle, size 9

75 cm (30 in) of 5 cm (2 in) wide French wired ribbon

For the impatiens spray

3 m (3 ⅓ yd) of 7 mm (¼ in) wide silk ribbon, Pink

5 m (5 yd 20 in) each of 4 mm (³⁄₁₆ in) wide silk ribbon: Pale Pink, White, Pale Blue

2 m (80 in) of 4 mm (³⁄₁₆ in) wide silk ribbon, Yellow

DMC Stranded Cotton, Grey/Green

Piecemaker tapestry needle, size 22

Piecemaker crewel needle, size 9

75 cm (30 in) of 4 cm (1 ⅝ in) wide French antique ribbon

METHOD

See the embroidery designs on page 117.

For all the sachets

1 Overlock or zigzag the edges of the silk, as it frays very quickly

2 Fold the dupion silk in half to mark the base line of the sachet. Secure the fabric in the embroidery hoop. Following the stitch guide below, commence the embroidery the distance above the base line indicated for each sachet: Canterbury bells, 2.5 cm (1 in); impatiens spray, 4.5 cm (1 ¾ in); pansy, 3 cm (1 ⅛ in); rose bowl, 1.5 cm (⅝ in).

TO COMPLETE

When the embroidery is completed, fold the sachet over double with the right sides together. Stitch down the sides. Turn the sachet through to the right side, taking care to push the corners right out. Fold the top of the sachet right in until it reaches the base line. Fill your sachet with lavender, then tie a beautiful bow.

STITCH GUIDE

Pansy Sachet

Pansies

Using 7 mm (¼ in) wide silk ribbon in the tapestry needle, make six straight stitch petals as shown.

Using the Black or dark contrast silk ribbon, make four small straight stitches.

OD = Overdyed Pink/Lemon
P = Pink
PP = Pale Pink

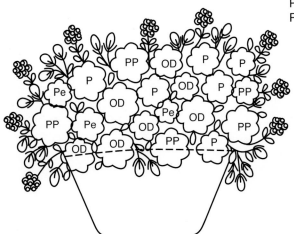

Rose bowl sachet

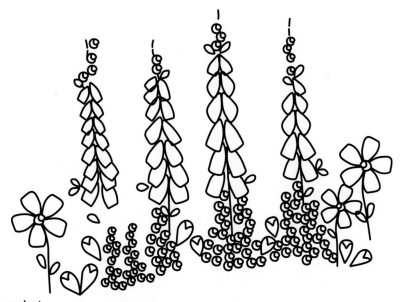

Canterbury Bells sachet

Impatiens spray sachet

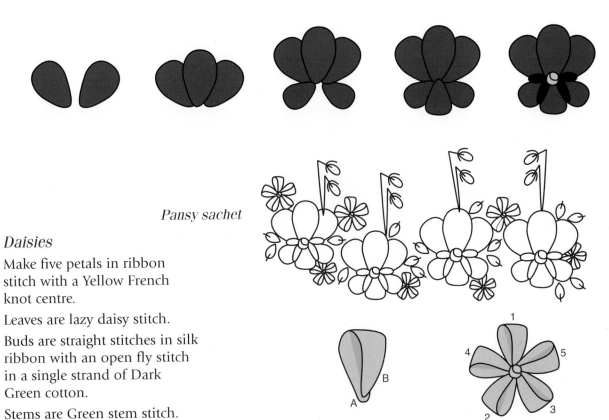

Pansy sachet

Daisies

Make five petals in ribbon stitch with a Yellow French knot centre.

Leaves are lazy daisy stitch.

Buds are straight stitches in silk ribbon with an open fly stitch in a single strand of Dark Green cotton.

Stems are Green stem stitch.

Rose Bowl Sachet

Roses are worked in overdyed and silk ribbons in fly stitch.

Buds are leaves are ribbon stitch.

Fillers are French knots.

Bowl outline is in stem stitch, using one strand of Light Tan cotton.

Other stems and buds are in open fly stitch, using one strand of Pale Green.

Canterbury Bells Sachet

Canterbury bells are worked in ribbon stitch, starting from 6 mm (¼ in) from the base of the stem and working up. Overlap the bottom three of four pairs as they get smaller.

Work three French knots at the top.

Stems are stem stitch using a single strand of cotton.

Leaves are lazy daisy stitch using a single strand of Dark Green cotton.

Mini-delphiniums are French knots, tapering upwards, worked in four shades of Mauve.

Daisies are ribbon stitch with a French knot centre.

Impatiens Spray Sachet

This flower has five petals which sit out from the fabric.

Using the 7 mm (¼ in) wide ribbon, bring the needle up from the back at A, then take it to the back at B leaving a petal of approximately 8 mm (⁶⁄₁₆ in) standing free. Hold that petal in your fingers when working the next petal. Work the five petals in the order shown. The centre is a Yellow colonial knot.

Stems are stem stitch in one strand of Grey/Green cotton.

Other stitches used, fly stitch roses, ribbon stitch buds, French knot forget-me-nots, colonial knot alyssum and lazy daisy leaves.

119

CHRISTMAS IS FOR GIVING

Christmas is for Giving

A Christmas gift that keeps on giving year after year, this embroidered picture is sure to be treasured by the recipient.

MATERIALS

35 cm (14 ¼ in) square of homespun cotton

Crewel needle, size 10

Straw needle, size 10

Small button

Small heart charm

Madeira Metallic Embroidery Thread, 3004

Stranded Cotton:

DMC	Maderia
502	1703
3045	2103
White	White
781	2213
3362	0601
315	0810
902	1601
550	0714

Water-soluble marker pen

Note: This piece has been worked in Madeira Stranded Cotton.

PREPARATION

See the tracing and embroidery designs on this page and 124. Trace the outline and the embroidery design using a water-soluble marker pen. All the embroidery is worked in one strand unless stated otherwise.

1 Using the crewel needle and 2103, back stitch around the bow. Satin stitch the bow in 2103, then satin stitch the inside of the bow in 2213.

2 Using the straw needle, embroider the roses on the swag, using 0601 for the centres and 0810 for the outer petals. Embroider the leaves as six bullions in three sets of two each in 1703. Fill in around the roses and leaves with tiny French knot flowers in 2103. There are five French knots of two twists around the needle in a close circle with a French knot in 1703 in the centre.

3 Using the straw needle, embroider the roses and leaves around the heart and fill in with tiny French knot flowers.

4 Link the heart to the bow with tiny chain stitches in 2103; link the stockings to the swag in the same way.

5 Using the crewel needle, outline the stockings in tiny back stitches in 0601. The stocking on the right has a top embroidered with French knots of two twists around the needle in White, using the straw needle. The stocking on the left has a satin stitch top in 0601, using the crewel needle.

6 Embroider the patterns on the stockings, following the embroidery diagram and key.

7 Using the crewel needle, embroider the tassels at the bottom of the heart and the ends of the swag in 2103.

Christmas is for giving

Bullion rose buds

Bullion roses

Satin stitch

French knot flowers

Tassels

from the heart

⊔⊔⊔⊔⊔⊔	Blanket stitch
⊤⊤⊤⊤⊤⊤	Blanket stitch with French knot
⟩⟩⟩⟩⟩	Fly stitch
○○○○○○	Chain stitch
×××××	Cross stitch
✻ ✻ ✻	Stars
৶৽৶৽	French knots
৶ ৶	Rose buds

8 Using the crewel needle and 0601, embroider the motto using tiny back stitches. Try to use your own writing for the motto, it adds that personal touch.

MAKING UP

1 To age the piece and reduce the brightness of the fabric and the embroidery, dye it in tea or coffee, following the instructions on page 37.

2 Using the crewel needle and the metallic thread, carefully attach the button in the centre of the bow and the heart charm in the centre of the embroidered heart.

Christmas Stockings

MATERIALS

Exact fabric requirements will depend on the print you choose. Use 50 cm (20 in) of 115 cm (45 in) wide cotton of vertically striped fabric or 35 cm (14 ½ in) of 115 cm (45 in) wide all-over print cotton.

20 cm (8 in) contrasting cotton or felt

35 cm (14 ¼ in) lightweight wadding

Braids, ribbon, lace, bells and holly for trimming

1 Cut two stocking shapes each from main fabric and wadding. Cut two heels, two toes, two stocking tops. Cut two top facings from contrasting fabric or felt for fabric stocking. If using felt, scallop inner edges of contrast pieces by drawing around half shape of machine bobbin and cutting around outline.

2 Place wadding sections against wrong side of stocking pieces; baste. Baste contrast pieces into place, folding under any raw edges not covered by braid.

3 Stitch contrast pieces and any decorative braid into place. Scalloped felt pieces are stitched just inside scallops.

4 Place two stocking sections together with right sides facing. Stitch. Clip seams. Turn and press. For felt stockings, stitch around top again, trimming felt close to stitching.

5 For fabric stockings place top edge facings together with right sides facing. Stitch short ends. Place facing around stocking top with right sides together. Stitch around top edge. Turn facing to inside. Press. Neaten raw edge and handsew inside stocking.

6 Stitch loop of braid to heel side for hanging stocking.

7 Stitch your choice of Christmas trims into place, using our examples as a guide.

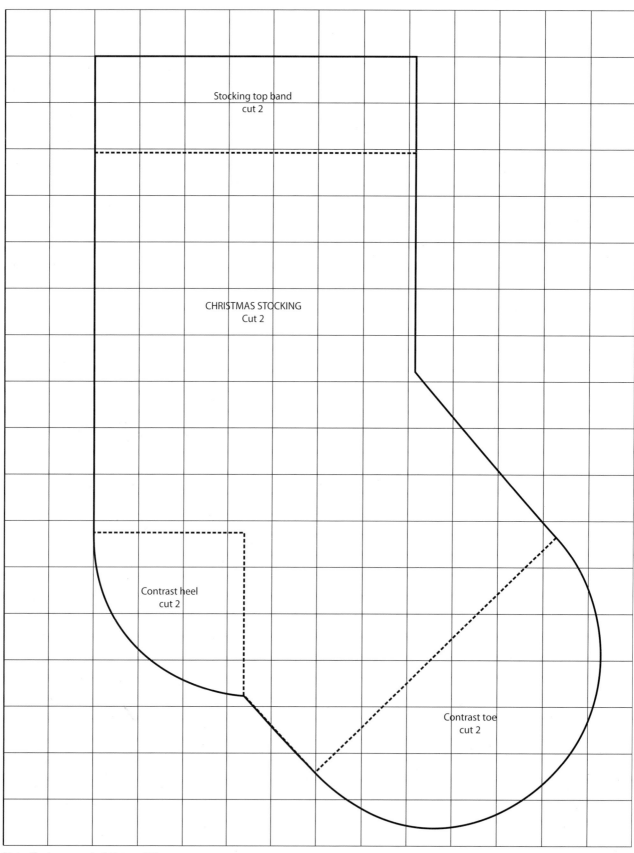

Stocking top band
cut 2

CHRISTMAS STOCKING
Cut 2

Contrast heel
cut 2

Contrast toe
cut 2

Note: Each square is 2.5 cm x 2.5 cm

Christmas Tree

A beautiful Christmas tree is the centre of family celebrations. Embroider your own tree, complete with tinsels, baubles and star.

MATERIALS

30 cm (12 in) square of cream homespun cotton

Crewel needle, size 10

Straw needle, size 10

Mill Hill small glass beads: Burgundy, Blue, Antique Gold

Madeira Metallic Embroidery Thread, Gold 3004

Brass charms (optional)

Embroidery hoop

Stranded Cotton:

DMC	MADEIRA
3362	1601
550	0714
781	2213
500	1705
898	2006

Note: This piece has been worked in Madeira Stranded Cotton.

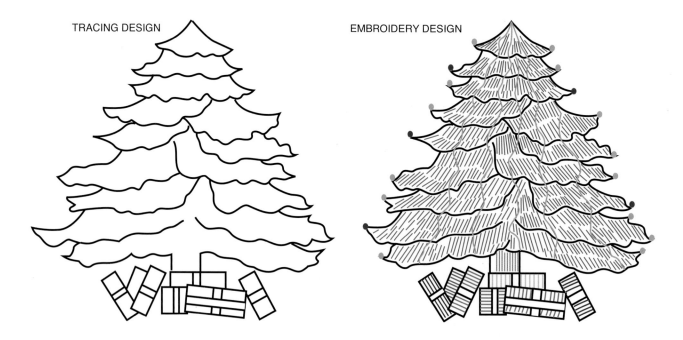

TRACING DESIGN

EMBROIDERY DESIGN

PREPARATION

See the embroidery and tracing designs on this page. Trace the design onto the fabric.

EMBROIDERY

Note: For the embroidery, follow the stitch guide on page 206. All the embroidery is worked in one strand unless otherwise stated.

1 Using the crewel needle and 1705, embroider the tree in long and short satin stitches, beginning at the top and working down. Refer to the design for the slope of the stitches.

2 Using the crewel needle, embroider the presents under the tree in satin stitch, using the photograph as a guide for the colours. Satin stitch the ribbons around the parcels in 3004.

3 Using the crewel needle, satin stitch the trunk of the tree in 2006.

Using the straw needle and 0714, 0601 and 3004, place a small French knot of one twist around the needle on the tip of each branch.

4 Using the crewel needle and 3004, back stitch the tinsel lines down the tree. Sew on the beads all over the tree, securing each bead with one or more beads at the bottom of the tree and among the presents.

Note: If you wish to age the piece by dyeing with tea or coffee, do it before the charms are attached.

5 Sew on the charms with the metallic thread. If you can't find a suitable star charm for the tree top, embroider one in 2213 with a double cross stitch.

Christmas Wreaths

MATERIALS

Wreath base purchased from florist or specialty shop

Variety of suitable trims such as holly leaves and berries, seed pods, nuts, artificial fruit, flowers and ribbons

Small loop wire for hanging

Spray paint, if desired

Hot melt glue gun or other suitable colourless craft glue

1 Spray paint wreath and allow to dry before decorating.

2 Plan layout for decoration before you begin to glue.

3 Prepare all trims—tie bows, spray paint nuts and gather small items into bunches.

4 Glue decorations into place.

5 Make a wire loop at centre back for hanging wreath.

Reindeer

MATERIALS

Pieces of wood about 3 cm
  (1 ⅛ in) thick and 5 cm
  (2 in) long for head;
  4 cm (1 ⅝ in) thick and
  10 cm (4 in) long for body;
  1.5 cm (⅝ in) thick and 7 cm
  (2 ¾ in) long for neck;
  1 cm (⅜ in) thick and 3 cm
  (1 ⅛ in) long for tail

Twigs for antlers

Scraps of leather or vinyl for ears

Four 10 cm (4 in) lengths of
  1 cm (⅜ in) thick dowelling
  for legs

Holly, berries, gold cord and other
  suitable Christmas decorations

Craft glue or hot-melt glue gun

Small drill

Black paint and small paintbrush

1 Drill small holes for antlers on top of head. Glue antlers into place.

2 Cut out ear shapes, glue into place under antlers.

3 Drill holes for legs. Position legs so that reindeer stands securely. Glue legs into place.

4 Glue head to neck. Glue neck to body.

5 Glue on tail at an angle.

6 Cut eyes out of white paper, paint in pupils. Glue on eyes.

7 Trim with Christmas decorations. Glue on cord for hanging.

KNITTING

Cardigan for all Seasons

Boys' and girls' cardigan in four sizes with duplicate stitch motifs denoting the seasons on the fronts; if you wish to knit in the designs work the back first and use it to judge placement of motifs. Use colours as shown or as desired.

To place embroidery

Count the squares on desired chart to place spacing of motif. Refer to duplicate stitch on page 134 and work embroidery with yarn needle and appropriate yarn.

Duplicate stitch

Duplicate stitch, sometimes called Swiss darning, is a simple but very effective technique for adding motifs to stockinette stitch without the many complications of intarsia knitting. We chose it to add the delightful motifs to our Cardigan For All Seasons. Finish the piece of knitting to be embroidered and press and block it as instructed. Study the chart carefully before you begin. Note that one square represents one stitch and that each separate colour is indicated by its own symbol. Following the chart and key, embroider the motif onto your knitting, using the technique shown in the diagrams below. Depending on the relative thickness of the knitting yarn and the embroidery yarn or floss, it is often a good idea to use the embroidery yarn doubled. Do not secure the embroidery yarn with knots, but weave the ends in on the wrong side.

Materials

Yarn: 5 ply pure wool crepe 50 g (2 oz) balls: 2 (2 ½, 3, 3 ½) balls colour A; 1 (1 ½, 1 ½, 1 ½) balls colour B; 1 (1, 1, 1 ½) balls colour C. ½ ball less each colour for a short-sleeved cardigan.

Notions: One pair each 3.75 mm (No. 9) and 3 mm (No. 11) knitting needles; cable needle; 6 buttons; 2 safety pins.

Tension

26 ½ sts and 36 rows to 10 cm (4 in) over st st, using 3.75 mm (No. 9) needles. It is important to knit a tension square and to work to the stated tension in order to obtain the required measurements. If your square is bigger use finer needles. If your square is smaller use thicker needles.

Special abbreviations

yrn = yarn around needle: take yarn over, then to front of right hand needle making an extra loop

C2sl = slip next st onto cable needle and keep it in front of work, pass right hand needle point in front of next 2 sts, keeping sts on left hand needle, K1 in next sl st, then K1 into 1st missed st and drop it from left hand needle. Change colour and K1 into 2nd missed st and drop it from left hand needle, then K1 from cable needle.

Measurements

To fit underarm
 51 (56, 61, 66) cm
 20 (22, 24, 26) in
Garment measures
 56 (61, 66, 71) cm
 22 (24, 26, 28) in
Length
 30 (33, 37, 41) cm
 11¾ (13, 14 ½, 16) in
Long sleeve seam
 20 (23, 28, 33) cm
 8 (9, 11, 13) in
Short sleeve seam
 5 (5, 5, 5) cm
 2(2, 2, 2) in

Back

With 3 mm (No. 11) needles and 5 separate balls, cast on 8 (10, 11, 13) sts C, 11 (11, 12, 12) sts B, 36 (40, 42, 46) sts A, 11 (11, 12, 12) sts B, 8 (10, 11, 13) sts C. 74 (82, 88, 96) sts.

Using same colours as on needle, work in K1, P1 rib for 5 cm (2 in), ending with RS row.

Change to 3.75 mm (No. 9) needles and cont for patt as follows:

1st row: (WS) *purl to 2 sts before change of colour, (yrn) twice, P2, change colour, P1, (yrn) twice, rep from * 3 times more, purl to end.

2nd row: *Knit to 4 loops before change of colour, keeping yarn at back of work sl1 purlwise, then drop 2 extra loops, K1, change colour, K1, keeping yarn at back of work sl1 purlwise, then drop 2 extra loops, rep from * 3 times more, knit to end.

3rd row: *Purl to 2 sts before change of colour, sl1 purlwise, P1, change colour, P1, sl1

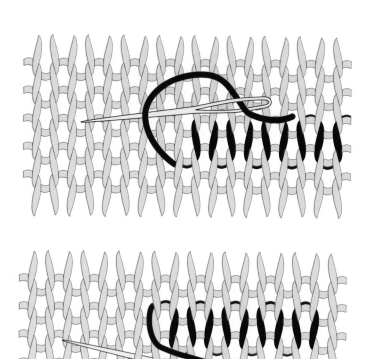

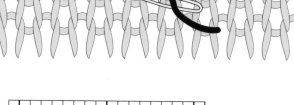

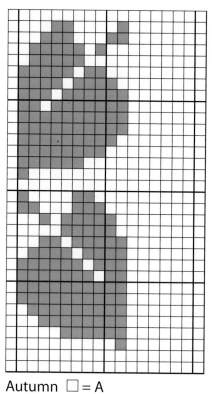

Autumn ☐ = A
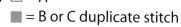
■ = B or C duplicate stitch

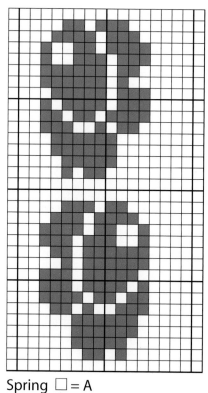

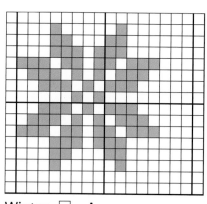

Winter ☐ = A
■ = B or C duplicate stitch

Spring ☐ = A
■ = B or C duplicate stitch

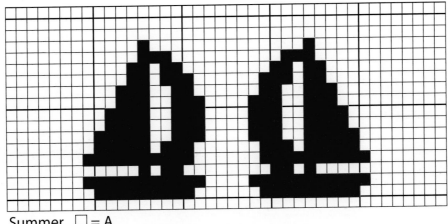

Summer □ = A
■ = B or C duplicate stitch

purlwise, rep form *3 times more, purl to end.

4th row: *Knit to 2 sts before change of colour, C2sl, rep from * 3 times more, knit to end.

5th, 6th rows: Using colours as on needle purl 1 row, then knit 1 row.

Rep last 6 rows for patt.

Cont in patt until work meas 18 (21, 23, 26) cm [7 (8 ¼, 9, 10 ¼) in] from beg, ending with WS row. Adjust length at this point if required, ending on WS row.

Shape raglans

Cast/bind off 4 (5, 5, 6) sts at beg of next 2 rows.

Next row: K2 tog, patt to last 2 sts, sl1, K1, psso.

Next row: Patt without dec.

Rep last 2 rows until 26 (28, 30, 32) sts rem, ending with WS row. Cast/bind off.

LEFT FRONT

With 3 mm (No. 11) needles and 3 separate balls, cast on 28 (30, 32, 34) sts A, 11 (11, 12, 12) sts B, 8 (10, 11, 13) sts C. 47 (51, 55, 59) sts. Using colours as set work 4 rows in K1, P1 rib.

For boys' cardigan:
Buttonhole row: Rib to last 7 sts, cast/bind off 3 sts, rib to end.

Next row: Rib and cast on 3 sts over buttonhole position.

For both boys' and girls' cardigans: cont in rib as before until 5 cm (2 in) from beg, ending with RS row.

Next row: Rib 10 sts and leave these 10 sts on safety pin for front band. Change to 3.75 mm (No. 9) needles. *Purl to 2 sts before change of colour, (yrn) twice, P2, change colour, P1, (yrn) twice, rep from * once more, purl to end. 37 (41, 45, 49) sts.

Cont in patt as set, working C2sl on foll 3rd row, then on every foll 6th row as for Back. Work until piece meas same as for Back to raglan shaping,

ending at side edge. Keeping patt correct, cont as follows:

Shape raglan

Cast/bind off 4 (5, 5, 6) sts at beg of next row. Work 1 row. Dec 1 st at raglan edge by working K2 tog on next and every foll 2nd row until 22 (23, 25, 26) sts rem, ending at front edge.

Shape neck

Cast/bind off at beg of next and every alt row 2 (3, 4, 4) sts once, 2 (2, 3, 4) sts once, 2 sts twice (all sizes). 1 st 3 times (all sizes), AT SAME TIME dec 1 st at raglan edge as before until 2 sts rem.

Work 2 sts tog, fasten off.

RIGHT FRONT

With 3 mm (No. 11) needles and 3 separate balls, cast on 8 (10, 11, 13) sts C, 11 (11, 12, 12) sts B, 28 (30, 32, 34) sts A. 47 (51, 55, 59) sts. Using colours as set work 4 rows in K1, P1 rib.

For girls' cardigan: Buttonhole row: Rib 4 sts, cast/bind off, rib to end.

Next row: Rib and cast on 3 sts over buttonhole position.

For both boys' and girls' cardigans: Cont in rib as before until 5 cm (2 in) from beg, ending with RS row. Change to 3.75 mm (No. 9) needles.

Next row: *Purl to 2 sts before change of colour, (yrn) twice, P2, change colour, P1, (yrn) twice, rep from * once more, purl to last 10 sts, leave rem 10 sts on safety pin for front band. 37 (41, 45, 49) sts. Cont to work as for Left front, reversing shapings.

LONG SLEEVES

With 3 mm (No. 11) needles and 5 separate balls, cast on

2 sts C (all sizes), 10 (10, 11, 11) sts B, 15 (17, 17, 19) sts A, 10 (10, 11, 11) sts B, 2 sts A (all sizes). 39 (41, 43, 45) sts.

Using colours as on needle work in K1, P1 rib for 5 cm (2 in), ending with WS row and inc st in each of B sections and 4 sts in A section on last row. 45 (47, 49, 51) sts. Change to 3.75 mm (No. 9) needles and beg with 6th row cont in patt as before AT SAME

TIME inc 1 st each end of 5th row once, then on every foll 6th row until there are 57 (63, 67, 73) sts, taking all inc sts into C sections.

Count on these sts in patt without further inc until Sleeve meas 20 (23, 28, 33) cm [8 (9, 11, 13) in] from beg, ending with WS row. Adjust length at this point if required, ending with WS row. Keeping patt correct, shape raglans as for Back until 9 sts (all sizes) rem. Work 1 row. Cast/bind off.

SHORT SLEEVES

With 3 mm (No. 11) needles and 5 separate balls, cast on 6 (8, 9, 11) sts C, 9 (9, 10, 10) sts B, 17 (19, 19, 21) sts A, 9 (9, 10, 10) sts B, 6 (8, 9, 11) sts C. 47 (53, 57, 63) sts. Using

colours as on needle work in K1, P1 rib for 7 rows. On 8th row, working in rib, inc 2 sts in each of 5 sections. 57 (63, 67, 73) sts.

Change to 3.75 mm (No. 9) needles and beg with 6th row cont in patt as before until Sleeve meas 5 cm (2 in) from beg, ending with WS row. Adjust length at this point if required ending with WS row. Keeping patt correct, shape raglans as for Back until 9 sts (all sizes) rem. Work 1 row. Cast/bind off.

TO MAKE UP

Sew in all ends. Press lightly on wrong sides. Matching colours, sew all 4 raglan seams. Sew up side and Sleeve seams.

BAND

Transfer 10 sts from safety pin on right front for boys or on left front for girls onto 3 mm (No. 11) needles. Rejoin A at inner edge, inc 1 st in first st, rib to end. 11 sts. Cont in rib as before until Band, slightly stretched, fits neck edge, ending with WS row and dec 1 st at end of last row. 10 sts. Leave 10 sts on safety pin. Sew Band in place.

Mark off 6 buttonhole positions. First one is already made, 6th one will be on 4th and 5th rows of neckband, 4 others are evenly spaced between.

BUTTONHOLE BAND

Work as other Band making buttonholes as marked.

NECKBAND

With RS facing, 3 mm (No. 11) needles and A, K10 over right front band, pick up and knit 19 (19, 21, 21) sts on right front neck, 7 sts (all sizes) on sleeve top, 31 (33, 33, 35) sts on back neck, 7 sts (all sizes) on sleeve top, 19 (19, 21, 21) sts on left front neck, K10 over left front band, 103 (105, 109, 111) sts.

Change to B and purl 1 row. Cont in K1, P1 rib for 8 rows AT SAME TIME make a buttonhole on foll 3rd and 4th rows as before. Cast/bind off in rib.

TO FINISH OFF

Using wool sewing needle and contrast colour as illustrated, embroider motifs onto fronts from graph as desired. Sew on buttons.

Cap

MATERIALS

Yarn: 5 ply pure wool crepe 50 g (2 oz) balls: 1 ½ balls slate green (A); small quantity sandy brown (B) and natural (C).

Notions: set of four 3.75 mm (No. 9) knitting needles; one 2.8 cm (1 ⅛ in) self-cover button for top; two 2 cm (¾ in) self-cover buttons for chin strap.

MEASUREMENT

To fit head 48 cm to 51 cm (18 ½ in to 20 ¼ in).

EAR PIECE

With 2 needles from set of 4 and A, cast on 11 sts.

1st row: K1, (P1, K1) 5 times.

2nd row: P1 (K1, P1) 5 times.

Rep last 2 rows twice.

7th row: (K1, P1) twice, (K1 in front and back of loop) in each of next 3 sts, (P1, K1) twice.

8th row: (P1, K1) twice, P6, (K1, P1) twice.

9th row: (K1, P1) twice, inc 1 st in next st, knit to last 5 sts, inc 1 st in next st, (P1, K1) twice.

10th row: (P1, K1) twice, purl to last 4 sts, (K1, P1) twice.

11th to 27th rows: Rep 9th and 10th rows 8 times, then 9th row once more. 34 sts*. Break off yarn. Make another one the same to *, work one row, ending with RS row, then cont as follows:

Next row: With WS facing, (P1, K1) twice, purl to last 4 sts, (K1, P1) twice, with RS facing cast on 23 sts for back, facing WS of other ear piece work (P1, K1) twice, purl to last 4 sts, (K1, P1) twice.

Next row: (K1, P1) twice, K26, (P1, K1) 15 times, P1, K26, (P1, K1) twice.

Next row: (P1, K1) twice, P26, (K1, P1) 15 times, K1, P26, (K1, P1) twice.

Rep last 2 rows twice more, then with RS facing, using 4 needles as required, cast on 37 sts for front and with RS facing cont in rnds as follows:

1st rnd: (P1, K1) 20 times, P1, K26, (P1, K1) 15 times, P1, K26, (P1, K1) twice, 128 sts. Catch sts to join in rnd at this point. Rep 1st rnd 3 times.

5th rnd: (P1, K1) 20 times, P1, K83, (P1, K1) twice.

Rep 5th rnd 5 times.

11th rnd: Knit to end.

Rep 11th rnd until front section meas 12 cm (4 ¾ in) from cast-on edge.

SHAPE TOP

1st rnd: (K14, K2 tog) 8 times.

2nd and each alt rnd: Knit

3rd rnd: (K13, K2 tog) 8 times.

5th rnd: (K12, K2 tog) 8 times.

Cont to dec 8 sts evenly in this way, working 1 st less before each K2 tog on every foll 2nd rnd until 24 sts rem. Knit 1 rnd, then break off keeping length of yarn attached.

Thread end of yarn through rem 24 sts and draw up tightly and securely fasten off.

COVER FOR LARGER BUTTON

With 2 needles from set of 4 and B, cast on 10 sts. Work in st st, inc 1 st each end of 1st and 3rd rows. 14 sts.

Work 11 rows straight, then dec 1 st each end of next and foll 2nd row once more. Cast/bind off purlwise on next row.

COVER FOR SMALLER BUTTONS

With 2 needles from set of 4 and B, cast on 6 sts. Work in st st, inc 1 st each end of 1st and 3rd rows. 10 sts.

Work 5 rows, then dec 1 st each end of next and foll 2nd row once more. Cast/bind off purlwise on next row.

CHIN STRAP

With 2 needles from set of 4 and A, cast on 4 sts.

1st row: K4, then with RS facing push work to other end of same needle and take yarn across back of work to start next row. Always with RS of work facing, rep 1st row until piece meas 23 cm (9 in), then cast/bind off.

TO FINISH OFF

With C and a wool sewing needle, embroider motifs from graph around head and on each ear piece. Fold chin strap in half and sew together side by side, leaving looped end open for buttoning. Attach one end of strap to outside of ear piece. Attach one smaller button, through all thicknesses, over strap and other smaller button of other ear piece to match. Attach larger button to centre top.

HOME
DECORATING

Decorative Screen

Fabric covered screens can be made from any type of wood that is sturdy enough to support its own weight.

BEFORE YOU BEGIN

If you wish to shape the top of the screen, you will need a jigsaw and a paper pattern to follow when cutting.

MATERIALS

Large sheet of paper

Pencil

3 panels of craft wood, each 16 mm x 50 cm x 1.6 m (⅝ in x 20 in x 64 in)

Jigsaw

5 m (5 yd 20 in) of 120 cm (48 in) wide fabric

1.3 m (52 in) of 1–1.5 cm (⅜–⅝ in) wide braid

10 m (11 yd 4 in) of 60 cm (24 in) wide polyester wadding or 5 mm (¼ in) thick foam

6 brass hinge brackets and screws

Screwdriver

Scissors

Use a screen to divide a room, provide a private space or hide what you don't want to be seen!

Wood glue
PVA adhesive
Spray adhesive
Staples and staple gun, or
    upholstery tacks

METHOD

1 Make a paper pattern for the curved top of the screen panels. Using the pattern, mark the curve in pencil on top of each panel of craft wood, then cut it out with a jigsaw.

2 Cut two pieces of fabric, each 55 cm x 1.6 m (22 in x 64 in) for each panel. Cut two pieces of wadding or foam, each 50 cm x 1.6 m (20 in x 64 in). Using the spray adhesive, glue the wadding or foam to the front and back of each panel.

3 Lightly spray the adhesive on to the wadding, then lay the fabric on top, trimming the top edge in the curved shape of the wood panels with a 2.5 cm (1 in) allowance.

4 Staple or tack the fabric edges in place. Trim away the excess fabric.

5 Starting at the bottom, turn in the end of the braid, staple or tack it over the fabric edge, then proceed to glue the braid all around each panel, covering the raw edge of the fabric. At the other end, turn under the raw edge of the braid and staple or tack it in place.

6 Attach the hinges. The first hinge should be approximately 20 cm (8 in) from the bottom and the other hinge should be approximately 20 cm (8 in) from the top of the screen.

Stencilling

Stencilling is one of the oldest decorative effects and can be as simple or ornate as you wish. Traditionally, stencils were cut from oiled cardboard or even brass sheets and were regarded as a craftsman's tools. Today you can still use brass and cardboard stencils but inexpensive plastic stencils are now readily available in an enormous variety of contemporary and traditional designs. You can also design and cut your own stencil using a plastic sheet and tracing your chosen design with a chinagraph pencil or a fine, indelible, felt-tipped pen.

BEFORE YOU BEGIN

It is important to use the correct brush for stencilling — an ordinary paint brush will not do. Stencil brushes are flat-topped are used by dabbing the brush down onto the area to be coloured, rather than stroking. This prevents paint being pushed under the stencil edges and smearing the design. You can use small natural sponges.

As for your paints, it is best to use acrylic or special fast-drying stencil paint. If mixing colours to achieve a desired tint, mix enough for the entire room, as it is difficult to duplicate a particular colour

mix. Take care too that your paints are very creamy in consistency, so they will not clog the brush or sponge, but not so thin that they will run under the stencil edges. If you are stencilling in more than one colour and are concerned that the colours should not run into one another, paints can be dried quickly with a hairdryer on low force and medium heat.

If stencilling with more than one colour, it is a good idea to cover with masking tape those parts of the stencil design to be painted in the second colour. Wait for the first colour to dry

Applying the first colour of the stencilled border to the wall.

Applying the second colour to complete the stencilled design.

before stencilling with the second one and so on. This will stop one colour from bleeding into the other.

Stencilling a border

MATERIALS

Suitable paint
Stencil brushes
Manila cards
Linseed oil
Mineral turpentine (white spirit)
Sharp craft knife
Cutting board
Pencils
Plumb line
Spirit level
Chalk
Masking tape

METHOD

To make the stencil, generously coat both sides of appropriately sized manila card with a 50:50 mixture of linseed oil and mineral turpentine (white spirit) and allow to dry. Remove any excess oiliness by wiping with a soft cloth. Cut out your pattern with the sharp craft knife.

1 Paint the wall in the normal way. Then, using a plumb line and spirit level, mark the position of your border, marking both horizontal and vertical base line.

Use this stencil design at any size you like. Simply enlarge it on a photocopying machine to your preferred size

144

2 Place the stencil on the wall, aligning its edges with the drawn lines and marking each corner of the stencil with easily-removed blackboard chalk. Continue placing the stencil along the guidelines, marking the corners along the entire length of the border.

3 Attach the stencil to the wall with masking tape. If you are using more than one colour, cover over any areas to be painted in another colour with masking tape to avoid paint overlapping.

4 Be sure to remove any excess paint from your brush or sponge before applying it to the wall. You will find surprisingly little paint is needed. Work in circular movements from the centre of each cutout area to the edges. Part of the charm of a stencilled decoration is the variations that occur in paint application, so don't feel compelled to paint until a solid block of colour appears, or to match one motif exactly to the next.

5 When the paint is dry, unmask the stencil and clean it if necessary. Then move the stencil to the next set of chalk marks and paint as before. Continue in this way until the border is completed.

Wall Finishes

SPONGING

This is one of the quickest and easiest ways of achieving a broken colour effect on walls and woodwork. Your base coat should be emulsion or acrylic paint in a light colour. Your second and subsequent colours are either brighter or darker and are applied by dabbling all over the base coat with a large natural sponge. You can use several tones of the one colour for a subtle finished effect. If you intend to sponge several rooms with different colours, it is a good idea to keep one sponge for each colour. Do not use paint directly from the paint tin. Pour a small amount into a shallow tray to prevent the sponge becoming overloaded with paint.

RELIEF PAPER

This traditional wallpaper has a long decorative history. The paper is pressed over rollers leaving an all over raised pattern which stays permanently in place. The thickness of the paper makes it ideal for disguising any imperfections in walls, and is the ideal treatment for the area between traditional chair rails (dado) and skirting boards. Once the paper is dry, paint it to match or contrast with the rest of the room. Relief papers are mostly inexpensive and are not pre-pasted.

RAGGING

This is a very quick and effective way to achieve an

Applying the base coat in a random pattern, using a sponge.

Applying the second coat with a fresh sponge.

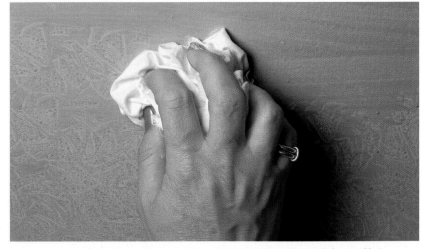

The process of ragging showing the darker paint being lifted off the lighter one with a scrunched-up rag, leaving behind the ragging effect.

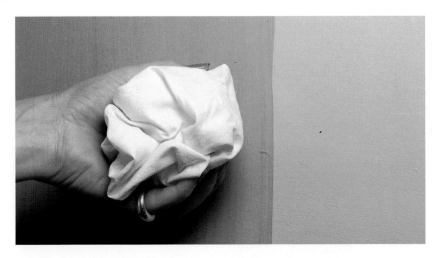

enough of the base coat will show through after ragging. Just after the top coat is applied, it is 'lifted off' by dabbing with a rag or something similar, exposing the base colour and creating an interesting crushed effect. The base coat can be of emulsion or acrylic paint or oil-based. Oil-based paints give a richer look than emulsion. For the top coat, use oil-based paint thinned with mineral turpentine (white spirit), emulsion or acrylic paint, thinned with water. You can contrast colours or tones of the same colour, by applying a top coat that is darker than the base.

interesting effect on a plain wall, using a scrunched-up, lint-free rag or even a plastic bag. You may find some team effort worthwhile here, as the effect depends on the top coat of paint being 'lifted off' just after it is applied. While one person is painting the top coat, the other member of the team can follow behind doing the ragging. If the top coat is allowed to dry too much, the effect will be spoiled as not

GENERAL CRAFTS

Gourmet Tassels

These tassels have a country feel and are ideal for decorating bottles of homemade vinegar, jars of preserves, jams or sauces. Decorated with a sprig of the appropriate herb, they make welcome gifts or you can use them to enhance your own kitchen. We have included a simple recipe for herb vinegar — so enjoy!

MATERIALS

Raffia

Dried lavender or dried herbs

White wine vinegar

Clear craft glue

Scissors

Hot glue gun

Decorative clear glass bottle with a cork

VINEGAR

Place the lavender flowers and leaves or fresh herbs to taste in the decorative glass bottle. Boil some white wine vinegar and, while it is still hot, pour it over the lavender or herbs. Allow the vinegar to cool, then seal the bottle with the cork. It is important that the bottle is airtight. Allow the vinegar to sit for several weeks to develop flavour before using it.

Large knot tassel

1 Make a plaited raffia strip long enough to loop around the neck of the bottle.

2 Tie a knot in the middle of a bundle of raffia, but before pulling the knot tight, loop one end of the raffia through the knot again, as if tying a non-slip knot. Thread the handle of plaited raffia through the knot (head of the tassel) and pull firmly.

3 Tie a band of raffia around the neck of the tassel, securing it at the back. Trim the tassel to the desired length. Decorate with heads of dried lavender and bunches of dried herbs.

4 Form a small wreath with the plaited handle which has been threaded through the knot, big enough to slide over the neck of the bottle. Wind it back on itself, until it is worked back to the head of the tassel, then using the hot glue gun, glue the raw edges down behind the head of the tassel.

5 Slide the circle of plaited raffia over the neck of the bottle. Position the tassel then hold it in place, using a small dob of hot glue. Apply the glue to the back of the tassel, then press it onto the bottle.

Large braided tassel

For the large braided tassel, make a plait of raffia and leave long loose ends to make the tassel fringe. Loop the plait around in a small wreath shape and wind it back on itself. Use a thinner plait of raffia to wrap around it, creating the neck of the tassel. Decorate it with sprigs of herbs. Slide the wreath over the neck of the bottle and secure it in place, using the hot glue gun.

Reclining Tassel

This tassel is simply achieved, using an ordinary household mop and some rope. It is ideal for tying back casual curtains or to enhance a cane chair, hammock or deck chair.

MATERIALS

Basic floor mop

1 m (40 in) of rope

1 m (40 in) of sash cord

Hot glue gun

METHOD

1 Cut enough rope to surround the base of the head of the tassel twice; the remaining length is used to create the hanger.

2 Coat the inside edge and the bottom of the plastic end of the mop with hot glue and insert both ends of the rope. This length can be adjusted, depending on the use for the tassel.

3 Using the hot glue gun, apply glue around the surface of the head of the mop. Starting from the bottom of the head, press the sash cord into the glue, winding it as you go; when you reach the top of the head, force the end of the cord into the hole for the handle.

4 Add the remaining rope around the bottom of the sash

cord ensuring that the ends meet and intertwine so there are no rough edges showing.

5 Add additional interest to

the tassel by tying knots in the cotton fibre around the top of the tassel.

Painted Silk Scarf

Silk painting, which is much easier than it looks, is not only a very satisfying hobby but also a wonderful source of presents for friends and family.

MATERIALS

Tracing paper and pencil

90 cm (36 in) square or 30 cm x 120 cm (12 in x 48 in) of plain silk (Habutai no. 8)

Silk frame

Silk pins

Masking tape

Clear gutta

Silk paints

Soft paintbrush

INSTRUCTIONS

See the design on page 154.

1 Enlarge the design from the pattern sheet to the required size to cover your piece of silk.

2 Stretch the length of silk over the frame, using special silk pins. Frames suitable for this purpose are available from craft shops, ready for you to assemble. A frame is essential for silk painting as it keeps the

The completed scarf.

Tracing the design.

Pinning the silk to the frame.

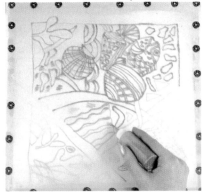

Outlining the design with the gutta.

silk quite taut and raised off the work surface.

3 Tape the design to the frame underneath the silk so that you can see it clearly through the fabric. Trace the main outlines with the pencil.

Painting the design.

4 Follow the pencil lines with the gutta (a gum-like material which serves to separate areas of colour, preventing one colour from bleeding into another). For the gutta to be effective the line must be continuous, any gaps will allow the silk paint to seep through. Allow the gutta to dry for an hour before beginning to paint.

5 Apply the paints with a soft brush, applying the colour between the lines of gutta and letting the paint creep up to the lines. Clean the brush in water before dipping it in the next colour.

6 When the painting is complete and the paint is dry, you can fix the colours by one of the following methods: iron on the back of the silk, steam the silk in a pressure cooker or professional steamer, or use a combination of microwave and fixative. Be guided by the instructions on the paint bottles. Your scarf is now ready to hem.

Mediterranean Platter

Bring all the sunshine of the Mediterranean into your home with this brightly coloured platter.

This method of decorating is called 'resist painting' where a material (in this case the chinagraph pencil) prevents the paint from covering a certain area. To create this primitive design, you will need a mixture of glass and ceramic paints.

MATERIALS

Plain white platter

Glass paint, emerald green

Ceramic paints in four colours of your choice

Paintbrushes for applying the design and a larger one for the varnish

Chinagraph pencil

Soft dry cloth

Mineral turpentine

Ceramic varnish

INSTRUCTIONS

1 Practise drawing the fish motif on a scrap of paper until you are happy with it, then using the chinagraph pencil, draw the design on to the platter. Those areas that are

The completed platter.

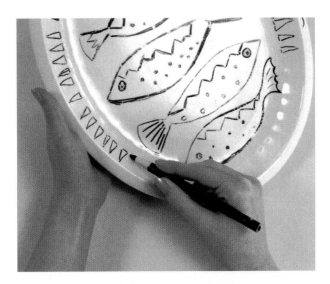

Drawing the design with a chinagraph pencil.

Painting the design with ceramic paints.

Cleaning off the chinagraph pencil.

Applying a coat of ceramic varnish.

covered with the chinagraph will remain white on the finished platter.

2 Carefully paint in the fish with the ceramic paints. Keep the colours bright with a strong contrast such as deep blue and yellow, purple and orange, or black and gold.

3 Paint the border pattern in another pair of bright colours such as red and blue. Don't try to be too neat. This primitive style lends itself quite well to a little irregularity.

4 Paint the water around the fish in emerald green glass paint, applying the paint in a wave pattern to indicate water and waves. Use glass paint for this part of the design as it is more translucent than ceramic paint.

5 When the paint is completely dry, rub off the chinagraph line with the soft dry cloth to reveal the white china beneath.

6 If you need to tidy up the edges of the platter, use the soft cloth soaked in mineral turpentine.

7 To protect your platter, paint it with a coat of ceramic varnish.

Sophisticated Glasses

The completed glasses.

MATERIALS

Scrap paper

Pencil

Wine glasses

Glass paint in the colours of your choice

Fine paintbrush

INSTRUCTIONS

1 Before you begin painting, it is a good idea to plan your design on some scrap paper. Don't be too restricted by this plan, just use it to decide what works well and what doesn't.

2 Using the fine paintbrush, begin working from either the top or the bottom of the glass, painting a winding vine around the bowl and stem. To ensue that the paint does not smudge while you are working, allow one area to dry before beginning the next one.

Painting in the design of the vines and leaves.

Country Garden Collage

The warmth of terracotta, combined with a posy of dried flowers is very appealing. Attached to weathered board, it has a truly rustic feel.

MATERIALS

Fence post framed board approximately 45 cm x 50 cm (18 in x 20 in)

Two terracotta half-pots, 9 cm (3 ½ in) diameter

Dry foam

Dried flowers, such as larkspur, safflower, lavender, daisy

Dried bud green foliage

Sphagnum moss

Mushrooms

Raffia

Glue gun

Lichen (optional)

ASSEMBLING

Step one

Cut the foam to fit the half-pots, then glue the pots and foam to the board.

Step two

Working on the right-hand pot first, place the lavender in the middle of the foam to form a stack with varying heights. Place moss around the base of the lavender to cover the foam.

Step three

Make a small bow from the raffia and glue it at the base of the lavender.

Step four

Glue the mushrooms at the side of the pot.

Step five

For the left-hand pot, place the dried bud green foliage at the back of the pot, graduating to either side of the pot in an A-shape. Place the safflower in between. Fill in with daisy and larkspur, making sure to use small pieces so as not to make the arrangements too heavy looking.

Step six

Tie another raffia bow and glue it to the front of the pot. For an extra rustic effect, glue lichen to the frame.

Scarecrow Hedge

A cheeky scarecrow guards this arrangement of dried cottage flowers from marauding birds.

MATERIALS

Fence post container approximately 12 cm x 35 cm (5 in x 14 in)

One bunch each of larkspur, lavender, pink daisies (dried)

Four hydrangea stems

Ten to twelve dried roses

Gum twigs with leaves

20 cm (8 in) scarecrow

Dry foam to fit the container

40 cm (16 in) piece of rope or twine

Glue gun

Fine wire

MAKING UP

1 Cut the foam to suit the box, then glue the foam into the box.

2 Starting at the back of the foam, layer 30–35 cm (12–14 in) pieces of larkspur and lavender together. Start in the middle, working out to the sides, stopping approximately 5 cm (2 in) from the outer edge.

3 Cut the roses approximately 5–7 cm (2–2 ¾ in) shorter than the lavender. Place the roses in front of the previous row, taking the roses around the sides to the back of the box.

4 Place the daisies in the same way as the roses, leaving space on one side to glue in the scarecrow.

5 Cut the hydrangeas into flowerettes and place them around the top of the box, taking them around the sides. Fill in the spaces at the back with the leftover hydrangeas and gum twigs. Twist the rope into a bow and attach with the fine wire.

Hat Boxes

Hat boxes provide excellent storage for a variety of bits and pieces.

BEFORE YOU BEGIN

How much fabric and wadding you need will depend on the size of your box and whether you are covering it or just lining it. For our fabric-covered box, we used approximately 1.3 m (52 in) of 15 cm (6 in) wide fabric and 50 cm (20 in) of wadding for the lid. Allow an extra 1.5 cm (⅝ in) for turn-unders and overlaps around the edges of all the fabric and wadding, unless instructed otherwise.

MATERIALS

Sturdy box with a lid

One strip of cardboard, the width of the outer lip of the lid and the same length as the circumference of the outer lip

PVA adhesive

Spray adhesive

Small paintbrush to apply the adhesive

Sufficient fabric

Medium thickness polyester wadding

Strip of a complementary fabric, 20 cm x 90 cm (8 in x 36 in), for the bow (optional)

Braid, ribbon, masking tape or fabric to cover the joins.

METHOD

1 Cut one lid from the fabric, 2.5 cm (1 in) larger than the top of the lid all around. Cut

one lid from the wadding without any additional allowance. Cut one strip of fabric the circumference of the base by the depth of the box plus 5 cm (2 in). Cut one strip of fabric the circumference of

the lid by the depth of the lid plus 1 cm (⅜ in). Cut one strip of cardboard the circumference of the lid by the depth. Cut a circle of fabric for the base, 2.5 cm (1 in) larger all around than the base. Cut one base from the cardboard, without any additional allowance.

2 Glue the wadding on to the lid and centre the fabric piece on top. Clip into the 2.5 cm (1 in) allowance of the fabric. Glue the clipped allowance down onto the sides of the lid, pulling the fabric quite taut. Trim away any excess fabric.

3 Glue the strip of fabric for the side of the lid to the corresponding strip of cardboard with the 1 cm (⅜ in) allowance left free all around. Clip into the allowance, then glue the fabric on one long side and both short ends to the wrong side of the cardboard. Glue the fabric-covered cardboard strip to the outside lip of the lid.

4 Turn in and press one short end of the fabric for the side of the box. Place the fabric around the outside of the box with the turned end covering the raw end and a 2.5 cm (1 in) allowance at the top and the bottom. Glue into place. Clip into the allowance all around the top and the bottom.

5 Turn the allowance at the bottom of the box over on to the base. Glue into place. At the top of the box, turn the allowance to the inside of the box and glue the allowance into place on the inside.

6 Place the fabric circle for the base face down on a protected surface. Clip into the allowance for 2.5 cm (1 in) all around the fabric piece. Spray the wrong side of the fabric with adhesive. Place the corresponding cardboard circle on the adhesive and press down. Turn the clipped allowance on to the cardboard and stick it into place.

7 Spray the base of the box with adhesive and glue the fabric-covered cardboard circle on to the base, covering all the raw edges.

8 Cover the joins on the inside of the box with braid, ribbon, masking tape or fabric. Make a bow in the complementary fabric, if desired, and glue it to the lid of the box.

Fabric-covered Picture Frames

MATERIALS

Pieces of strong cardboard in desired size

Pieces of fabric and wadding in desired size

Clear craft glue or spray-on photographic glue

Strong scissors

Craft knife

Cutting board

Lace, bows and ribbons for trimming

METHOD

1 Cut out three shapes from cardboard—one for backing, one for centre piece and one which will have centre cut out to reveal picture. Cut a piece of cardboard for stand approximately 5 cm x 10 cm (2 in x 4 in).

2 Cover one side of backing piece with glue. Apply wadding to this side. Trim wadding to within 1 cm (⅜ in) of cardboard. Turn 1 cm (⅜ in) to other side, clipping curves and excess wadding at corners. Glue into place. Cover with fabric in same way.

3 Cover one side of centre piece with fabric in same way, omitting wadding.

4 Cut out centre of front section. Cover with glue, wadding and fabric as for backing. Take care to clip curves so that wadding and fabric will turn to wrong side without too much bulk.

5 Glue centre and backing pieces together with fabric sides outwards. Glue front section onto completed backing, with fabric side outwards and leaving top section unglued to allow picture to be inserted.

6 Cover stand with wadding and fabric. Bend 1.5 cm (⅝ in) at one end of stand. Glue this end to back of frame at a point which allows frame to stand properly. You may wish to add a length of ribbon between stand and frame for added stability.

Trimming notes: Take care when placing fabric to take best advantage of print. Pre-gathered lace is easier to use for trimming than flat lace.

Nostalgia Box

What better way to preserve your special keepsakes than with this lovely box.

MATERIALS

Wooden nostalgia box, frame and mat

Acrylic paint for the base coat

Paintbrush

Glue gun

Antiquing medium (optional)

Oil paint, Burnt Umber (optional)

Soft cloth

Antique laces

Assorted memorabilia: postcards, photographs, small teddy bears, dolls, trinkets, dried flowers, ribbons, locks of hair, lockets and so on

Note: You can seal your box by means of a glass front, fixed under the frame.

METHOD

1 Paint the inside and outside of the box with two coats of acrylic paint, allowing the paint to dry thoroughly between coats. Paint the frame in the same way as the box.

2 If you wish to antique the frame, gently rub a little of the Burnt Umber oil paint and the antiquing medium on the frame, using the soft cloth. Allow it to dry for five minutes, then, with a circular motion, wipe off the frame until you have an antique finish that you like.

3 Attach the lace background to the inside back of the box, using the glue gun. Arrange all the trinkets and memorabilia on the background and on the 'floor' of the box, beginning with the larger items and filling in with the smaller ones. To ensure that there are no blank spots, view the arrangement from all angles, then glue all the items in place.

4 To give added depth to the box, glue a piece of lace across the front of the mat at the top.

5 When you are happy with the arrangement, fix the frame into place across the front of the box.

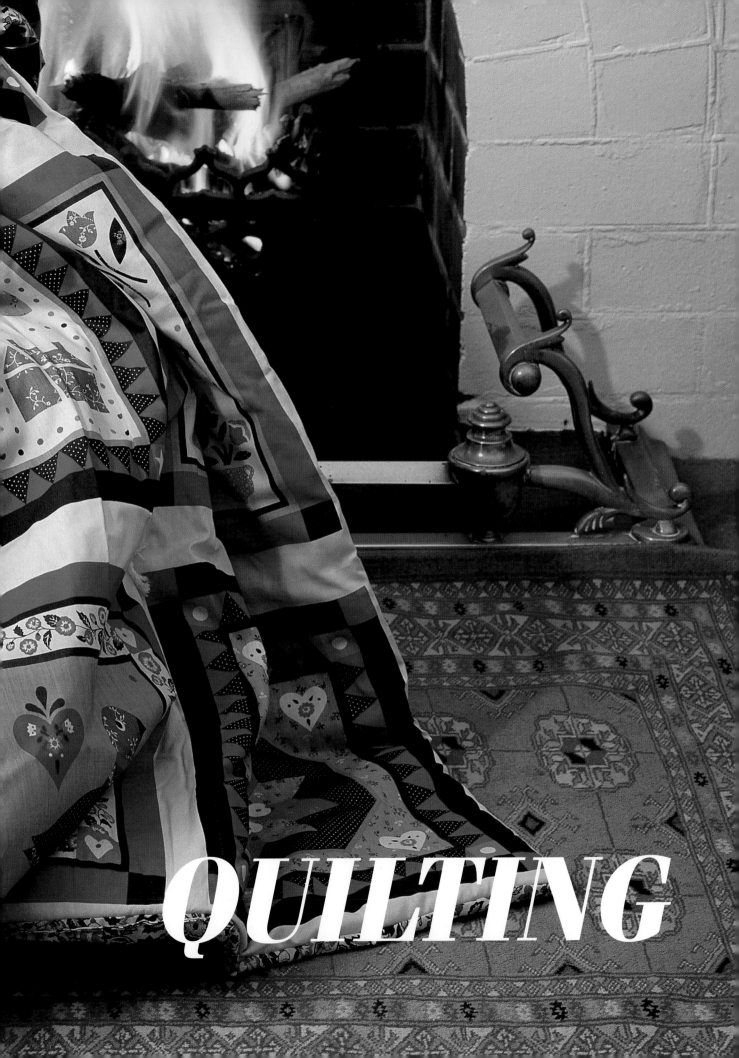

QUILTING

Quilter's Carry-all

For the quilter on the move—a large carry-all to hold a cutting mat, a quilter's ruler, a rotary cutter, a hoop and a large quilt.

The outside of the carry-all can be a printed panel, plain fabric or pieced with a block of your choice.

Finished size: 56 cm x 65 cm (22 ⅜ in x 26 in) when closed

MATERIALS

Pieced block (optional)

70 cm (28 in) of fabric for the outside

130 cm (52 in) of backing fabric

170 cm (68 in) of 74 cm (29 ½ in) wide thin wadding

160 cm (64 in) of polycotton fabric for the drawstring bag (can be the same as the backing)

100 cm (40 in) of polycotton fabric for binding and handles

40 cm (16 in) of fabric for the inside pockets

3 m (3 ¼ yd) of narrow cord

10 cm (4 in) of Velcro

Small quantity of polyester fibrefill

60 cm (24 in) of 12 mm (½ in) wide elastic

Two lengths of 12mm (½ in) thick dowel, each 65 cm (26 in) long

Four finials

Threads to match all the fabrics

METHOD

For the outside

1 If you are using a pieced block for the centre front or if you are piecing the whole front, do this first. Join the completed front to the fabric for the back, placing the seam at the spine of the carry-all. Pin the backing, wadding and fabric together for the entire outside of the carry-all as for the quilt. Hand- or machine-quilt in a design that suits the fabric or the block you have chosen.

In the carry-all photographed here, the front has been pieced, joined to the back and quilted. The centre block has been appliquéd on the front last of all, with narrow borders covering the edges of the block. If you are using a fabric panel with no piecing, pin the backing, wadding and the outside fabric together and quilt in an appropriate design.

2 Trim the piece to be 65 cm x 110 cm (26 in x 43 ¼ in) (Fig. 1).

For the cutting mat pocket

1 From the 160 cm (64 in) polycotton fabric, cut 52 cm x

Fig 1

70 cm (20 ⅞ in x 28 in) from one corner. Cut a piece of backing and a piece of wadding to the same size. Pin them together as for the outside of the bag, then quilt. Trim the piece to be 46 cm x 65 cm (18 ¼ in x 26 in). Baste the edges together.

2 Cut a 7.5 cm x 65 cm (3 in x 26 in) strip from the binding fabric. Press the binding over double with the wrong sides together. Stitch one edge of the binding along the top edge of the mat pocket with the right sides together, using a 6 mm (¼ in) seam. Fold half the binding to the wrong side. Turn under 6 mm (¼ in) on the raw edge and slipstitch it in place.

For the other pockets

1 Cut a total of 4.8 m (5 ⅓ yd) of 7.5 cm (3 in) wide strips for binding the pockets. Press the strips over double with the wrong sides together.

2 Cut a 40 cm x 65 cm (16 in x 26 in) piece for the ruler pocket. Fold it over double to measure 20 cm x 65 cm (8 in x 26 in). Cut a piece of wadding to the same size. Pin the wadding inside the doubled fabric. Quilt the pocket. Bind the top edge as for the mat pocket.

3 Cut a piece 10 cm x 22 cm (4 in x 8 ¾ in) for the rotary cutter pocket. Bind the top edge, turn under the other raw edges and stitch it on the inside of the mat pocket.

4 Cut two pieces 11.5 cm x 46 cm (4 ½ in x 18 ¼ in). Fold them over double to measure 11.5 cm x 23 cm (4 ½ in x 9 in).

Cut two pieces of wadding to the same size. Slip the pieces of wadding between the doubled fabric. Pin and quilt as before. Fold the binding over double again. Pin the binding to the side edges of each pocket with raw edges matching. Turn the folded edge of the binding to the back and slipstitch it down. Sew a piece of Velcro to the top of each pocket. Following Fig. 2, cut four flap sections from the fabric and two from the wadding. Pin the wadding between two fabric flaps. Quilt them as for the pockets. Bind them as for the side edges of the pockets. Sew a piece of Velcro to the underside of each flap to correspond with the Velcro on the pocket.

5 Cut a piece 22 cm x 65 cm (8 ¾ in x 26 in) for the centre pocket. Fold it over double to measure 22 cm x 32.5 cm (8 ¾ in x 13 in). Cut a piece of wadding to this size. Slip the wadding inside the doubled fabric. Pin and quilt as before. Bind the top edge as for the top edge of the mat pocket. Fold the binding over double again and bind the side edges as for the flap pockets.

6 Arrange all the pockets on the mat pocket, using the assembly diagram to guide you. For the flap pockets, note that the straight edge of the flap actually sits just below the top edge of the pocket so the

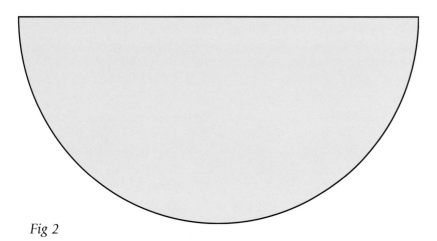

Fig 2

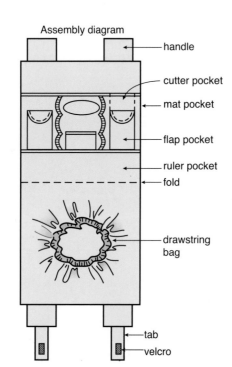

Assembly diagram

handle

cutter pocket

mat pocket

flap pocket

ruler pocket

fold

drawstring bag

tab

velcro

sufficient bias binding to go around the edge. Sew the bias binding around one piece with the raw edges matching. Sew a piece of Velcro to the centre of the other piece. Place the two pieces together with the right sides facing and the raw edges matching. Sew around the outside edge, leaving an opening for turning. Turn and stuff firmly with the fibrefill. Slipstitch the opening closed.

For the cotton reel holders

1 Cut two pieces of fabric, each 4 cm x 45 cm (1 ⅝ in x 18 in). Fold the fabric over double, lengthwise, with the right sides together. Stitch the long side and turn the tubes through to the right side.

2 Thread 30 cm (12 in) of elastic into each tube, securing the elastic at the ends of the tube with stitching, gathering the fabric up at the same time.
3 Turning under the raw ends, stitch the cotton reel holders in place as photographed, stitching through each one twice, making three separate compartments.

For the drawstring bag

Note: The drawstring bag on the pictured carry-all has been pieced with some of the pocket fabric for added interest. The instructions given here are for using a plain piece.

1 Cut the piece of fabric 43 cm x 160 cm (17 ¼ in x 64 in) and a second piece 43 cm x 82 cm (17 ¼ in x 32 ¾ in). Join these pieces together with narrow seams to make a large

flaps will need to be stitched in place first. Stitch the flaps down twice: once at the straight edge and again 12 mm (½ in) above. Stitch all the pockets in place in the stitching line of the binding. Sew on a piece of Velcro to attach the pin cushion to. Pin

the mat pocket to the inside of the front of the bag. Sew all the edges together.

For the pin cushion

Cut out two pieces of fabric in a sausage shape that is approximately 9 cm x 24 cm (3 ½ in x 9 ½ in). Make

tube 43 cm x 242 cm (17 ¼ in x 96 ⅞ in).

2 Make two buttonholes on opposite sides of the top, 3 cm (1 ¼ in) sewn from the top edge.

3 Make a casing at the top for the drawstring so that the buttonholes fall inside the casing. Thread the cord into the casing through the buttonholes and knot the ends.

For the handles

1 Cut four pieces of fabric, each 22 cm x 27 cm (8 ¾ in x 10 ⅝ in). Hem both long sides of each piece. Fold the pieces over double to measure 13.5 cm x 22 cm (5 ⅜ in x 8 ¾ in).

2 Cut four pieces of wadding 13.5 cm x 22 cm (5 ⅜ in x 8 ¾ in). Slip the wadding between the fabric layers.

3 Sew the sides of each piece up to 2.5 cm (1 in) from the folded edge. Quilt the handles, taking care not to stitch through the opening where the dowelling will pass through.

For the tabs

Cut two pieces, each 10 cm x 18 cm (4 in x 7 ¼ in). Fold each one over double, lengthwise, with the right sides together. Sew down the long side and one end. Turn and press. Sew a piece of Velcro to the closed end and a matching piece of Velcro on the back of the handles.

ASSEMBLING

1 Pin, then baste the drawstring bag on the inside of the carry-all with one edge on the centre fold.

2 Pin, then baste the mat pocket into place on the inside of the carry-all.

3 Cut a 7.5 cm (3 in) strip of fabric, 65 cm (26 in) long. Fold the strip over double and bind the join between the ruler pocket and the drawstring bag.

4 Cut sufficient 7.5 cm (3 in) wide straight binding to go all around the edges. Bind the side edges as before.

5 Sew the handles into position, placing the closed ends on the outside of the carry-all. Fold the handles to the inside of the carry-all with all the raw edges matching. Bind the top and bottom ends of the carry-all, catching the handles into the binding. Turn in the ends of the binding and slipstitch them closed.

6 Pass the dowelling through the handles. Attach the finials to the ends of the dowelling.

Crazy Patchwork

PIECING THE BASE CLOTH

Having decided on the fabrics you want to use, the next step is to piece the base cloth. There are several methods you can use, and the one you choose will be dependent to some extent on the type of project and its size.

RANDOM BLOCK

This is good for projects where any part is more than about 30 cm (12 in) square, and is quick and easy for beginners. It is not really suitable for fabrics that wriggle out of shape, like crepes or knits, unless they are interfaced.

1 Trace the pattern (if given) and cut two paper templates. If a pattern is not given, cut the piece(s) according to the dimensions given.

2 Depending on the size, rule three, four or fives lines on one template, dividing it into sections, and mark these with a felt pen (Fig. 1).

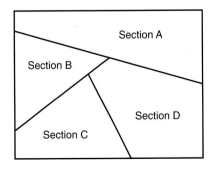

Fig 1

3 Divide these larger sections into smaller sections, making sure that you have no points where four lines meet. Aim for T intersections (Fig. 2).

Aim for T intersections rather than Xs

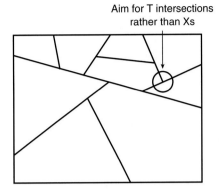

Fig 2

4 Determine the stitching order and label the parts A1, A2, A3, B1, B2, B3 and so on (Fig. 3).

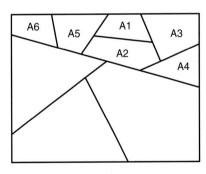

Fig 3

5 Now bring out your chosen fabrics and play around until you are happy with the combinations, remembering that you should not place a pattern next to a pattern (Fig. 4). Note which fabric is to be cut from each small template.

6 Trace a copy of the finished design onto the second paper template, then carefully cut one of the templates along the marked lines.

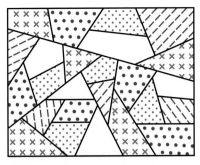

Fig 4

7 Cut out the fabric shapes, adding a 6 mm (¼ in) seam allowance on ALL the sides.

8 On the remaining template, lay out the fabric pieces, still attached to their paper shapes. Check that your combinations are working and that you don't have two pieces of the one fabric together or two patterns.

9 Returning to the decisions you made in step 4, stitch pieces A1 and A2 together, press the seam open, then add A3. Continue with each section until you have three, four or five large irregular-shaped blocks (as shown by the felt pen lines you drew in step 2).

10 Determine the order for stitching these irregular blocks, then stitch them together until the final shape is achieved. Stitch it round the edges onto a backing cloth and, if desired, baste along the lines sewn earlier in this step to hold it in place until the embroidery is far enough advanced to keep it stable.

FIVE-SIDED CENTRE PATCH

This is good for small pieces less than 30 cm (12 in) square. It is relatively quick, but there is greater fabric wastage than in the Random Block method.

1 Cut a piece of backing fabric 5 cm (2 in) larger all round than the size needed for the project. On the wrong side, mark the cutting line and stitching lines from the pattern.

2 Select the darkest of the fabrics you plan to use and cut out a rectangle, approximately 6 cm x 8 cm (2 ⅜ in x 3 in). Cut off one corner, making the rectangle a five-sided shape (Fig. 5).

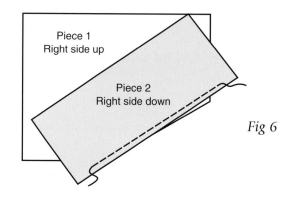

Fig 6

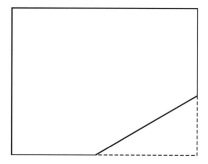

Fig 5

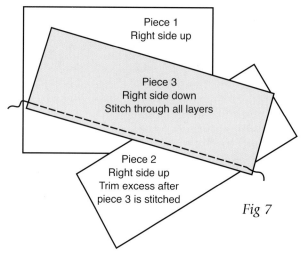

Fig 7

3 Cut a rectangle of another fabric approximately 6 cm x 8 cm (2 ⅜ in x 3 in), and pin the right sides together along the cut side of the first piece in the centre of the backing fabric (Fig. 6). Stitch the seam (through all three layers), then flip piece 2 right side up. Press the seam open.

4 Select the next piece of fabric and cut a strip 6 cm x 8 cm (2 ⅜ in x 3 in). Pin then stitch it in place, covering one raw end of pieces 1 and 2 (Fig. 7). Trim away any fabric behind the seam.

5. Continue to stitch on rectangles around the five-sided shape until all the edges are covered (Fig. 8). Your rectangles will increase in size as you go through each 'round'.

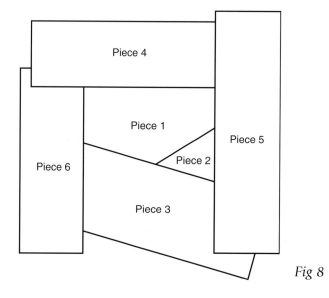

Fig 8

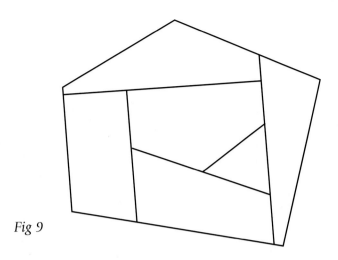

Fig 9

6 Now you have a larger piece of base cloth consisting of six fabrics. Shape this into a five-sided figure (Fig. 9).

7 Begin the next round of five fabrics in the same manner as before, reshaping the base cloth into a five-sided figure after each round. Be sure to trim any excess fabric from behind the seam and press each seam open carefully.

8 When the piecing is completed, machine-stitch a row of narrow, close zigzag stitches on the cutting line marked in step 1 and hand-stitch a row of basting stitches on the stitching line.

Bolster Cushion

A little added luxury for your bedroom or on a special chair in the lounge room, this bolster cushion is an eye-catcher.

MATERIALS

1 m (40 in) of fabric for the base cloth (also used to make the bolster insert)

Total of 55 cm x 60 cm (22 in x 24 in) of assorted fancy fabrics

20 cm x 90 cm (8 in x 36 in) of fancy fabric for the bolster ends

Two self-cover buttons, 5 cm (2 in) in diameter

20 cm x 40 cm (8 in x 16 in) of Vilene or other lightweight interfacing

40 cm (16 in) zipper to match the darkest fancy fabric

1.2 m (48 in) of piping to match the fabric for the bolster ends

Assorted embroidery threads, rayon and others

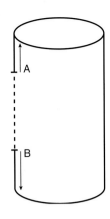

Fig 1

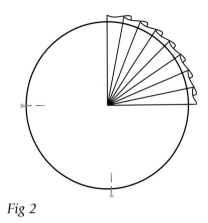

Fig 2

buttons to complete the decoration. Stitch a message if desired.

MAKING UP

1 Fold the bolster fabric with the right sides together. Stitch from A to the end, reinforcing the stitching at A with several back stitches. Stitch from B to the end, reinforcing at B with several back stitches (Fig. 1). Turn the piece right side out and insert the zipper in the opening.

2 Beginning at the seam, pin the piping over the hand-basting. Using the zipper foot, and stitching on top of the stitching on the piping (or as close to it as possible), apply the piping right round both ends of the bolster. Overlap the ends of the piping and trim them to 1 cm (³⁄₈ in). Leave the ends of the piping loose on the outside.

Two or three different laces or braids, totalling 1.5 m (60 in)

Buttons, beads, charms, etc

30 cm (12 in) each of four different colours of 3 mm (¹⁄₈ in) wide silk ribbons

Chenille needle

Crewel needles

Straw needle or a milliner's needle for grub roses

Ordinary sewing thread

Polyester fibrefill

Drawing materials

PREPARATION

Draw a rectangle 49 cm x 54 cm (19 ½ in x 21 ½ in) onto the wrong side of the base cloth fabric. Cut it out, allowing an additional 3 cm (1 ¹⁄₈ in) all round.

CRAZY PATCHWORK

1 Using the Random Block method, crazy patch the base fabric. On the wrong side, machine a row of zigzag stitches along the cutting line. Trim any excess fabric. Hand-sew a row of basting stitches on the stitching line.

2 Add lace or braids to cover some of the seam lines. Cover all the remaining seam lines with your choice of embroidery stitches. Embellish these rows of stitches with beads or stitch combinations of your choice. Do not bead past the row of hand-basting.

3 Add lace motifs, ribbon embroidery, tassels, beads and

3 From the Vilene or other interfacing, cut two circles, each 18 cm (7 in) in diameter. Cut the fancy fabric for the ends in half lengthwise, so each piece is 10 cm x 90 cm (4 in x 36 in). Join the short ends to make a circle. Fold the circle into quarters and mark the four points. Quarter each Vilene circle and mark the points. Pin the four points on the fabric circle to the four points on the Vilene circle. Pleat the fabric evenly in a fan-like manner to fit each quarter (Fig. 2). Aim to have the pleats deeper and sitting neatly over the top of one another in the centre. Stitch the pleats in place.

4 Cover the buttons and stitch them into place over the centre of the pleated ends, stitching through all layers.

5 Open the zipper and turn the bolster to the wrong side. Placing the fabrics with the right sides together, fit the pleated circles into the ends of the bolster. Using the zipper foot, stitch exactly over the piping stitching. Clip the curves, press the seams open carefully and turn the bolster to the right side.

6 For the bolster insert, cut a 53 cm (21 ⅛ in) square and two circles 18 cm (7 ¼ in) in diameter from the remaining base cloth fabric. Stitch the square to form a tube, leaving a 20 cm (8 in) opening in the seam. Insert the circles in the ends. Clip the curves, press the seams open and turn the insert right side out. Fill the insert with polyester fill and slipstitch the opening closed.

Insert the bolster into the cover and close the zipper.

Crazy Quilt Purse

This lovely patchwork purse has been richly embellished with embroidery, sequins, special buttons and charms. Adding your own embellishments to the basic design will make it unique to you.

Finished size (closed): 14 cm x 18 cm (5 ½ in x 7 ¼ in)

MATERIALS
Scraps of silk, satin and cotton fabrics

30 cm (12 in) of velvet, ultrasuede or heavy moiré or other suitable fabric

18 cm x 30 cm (7 ¼ in x 12 in) of homespun

18 cm x 30 cm (7 ¼ in x 12 in) of iron-on interfacing

30 cm (12 in) Pellon

Silk buttonhole twist or embroidery floss in an assortment of colours

Metallic threads

Beads, buttons, brass charms

3 m (3 ¼ yd) each of cord in four or five assorted colours and thickness

Three large buttons

Water-soluble marker pen

Tacky glue

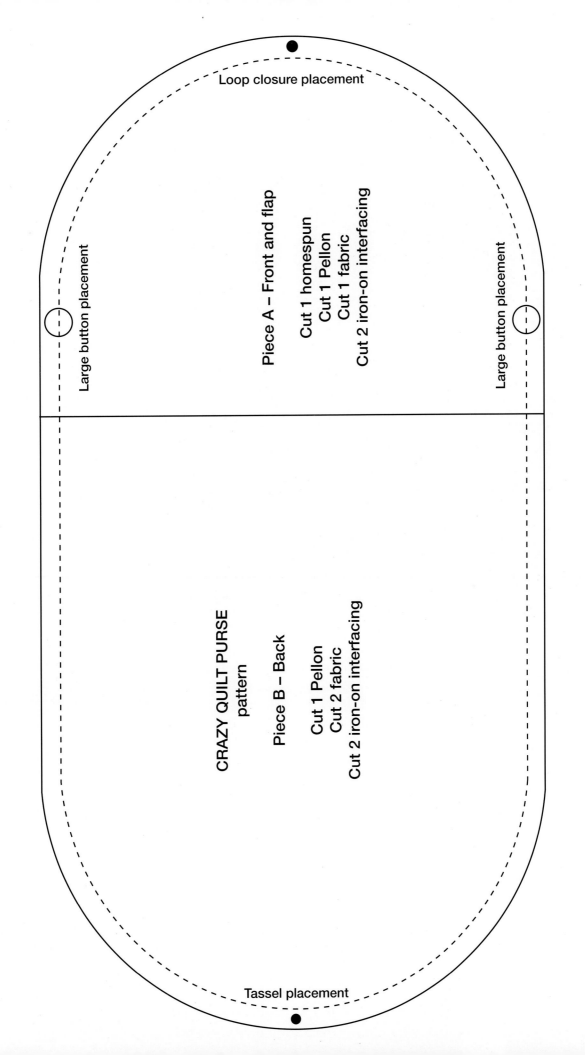

Loop closure placement

Large button placement

Piece A – Front and flap

Cut 1 homespun
Cut 1 Pellon
Cut 1 fabric
Cut 2 iron-on interfacing

Large button placement

CRAZY QUILT PURSE
pattern

Piece B – Back

Cut 1 Pellon
Cut 2 fabric
Cut 2 iron-on interfacing

Tassel placement

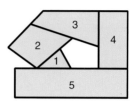

Fig 1

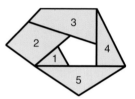

Fig 2

Continue to add pieces, keeping a balance of colour, texture, prints and plains.

5 When the homespun is covered, place pattern piece A over it and mark the shape with the water-soluble pen.

6 Stitch assorted laces and ribbons onto the patchwork piece. Cover all the seam lines with embroidery stitches, following the stitch guide on page 206, then sew on the beads, buttons and charms.

ASSEMBLING

1 Fuse the interfacing to the wrong side of the patchwork piece, the wrong side of the velvet, ultrasuede or moiré piece A and the wrong side of the velvet piece B.

2 Lay the velvet piece A on the table, facing upwards. Place the quilted piece on top, face down, then the Pellon. Pin the layers together. Stitch around the edge in a 1 cm (³⁄₈ in)

METHOD

See the Pattern on page 179.

1 Cut out the pattern pieces from the homespun, interfacing and velvet, ultrasuede or moiré as instructed on the pattern.

Note: When cutting pattern piece A from the homespun, allow an additional 12 mm (½ in) all around. This piece will be trimmed after all the embellishments are added.

2 Begin creating the patchwork from the centre of the piece. From a dark solid fabric, cut a five-sided shape. Pin it to the

approximate centre of the homespun piece A.

3 From another fabric, cut a rectangle that will cover an edge of the centre piece. Lay this piece on the centre piece with the right sides together and stitch in a 6 mm (¼ in) seam. Trim the seam allowance back to 3 mm (⅛ in). Press the rectangle back.

4 Working clockwise around the centre piece, continue adding rectangles until each side of the centre piece has been stitched (Fig. 1). Trim the free edges to create new angles and five new sides (Fig. 2).

seam, leaving a 5 cm (2 in) opening on one side. Trim the seam allowance, then turn the piece through to the right side. Slipstitch the opening closed. Press.

3 Place the two velvet pieces B together with the right sides facing and a piece of Pellon on top. Pin, stitch, turn and press as for the A piece.

4 Whipstitch the front and back together as shown on the pattern.

5 Whipstitch a length of cord along the edge of the flap, making a loop in the centre for the closure.

6 Braid the rest of the cords together to make a 140 cm (56 in) length. Tie the ends together, leaving approximately

5–8 cm (2–3 in) below the knot for a tassel.

7 Lay a narrow bead of glue around the edge of the purse. Pin the cord over the glued edge with the tassel at the bottom. Allow the glue to dry, then whipstitch the cord into place.

8 Sew one button at each side of the top and one button to close the purse.

Wool Quilt

This bed quilt is made from woollen fabrics in rich, warm tones, add wadding later if you prefer a warmer quilt.

MATERIALS

3.2 m (3 ½ yd) of 240 cm (96 in) wide calico for the base cloth and the backing

1 m (40 in) of red velvet or velveteen for the sashes and border or 1.8 m (2 yd) if you prefer not to have joins

Total of 1.5 m (60 in) of scraps of woollen fabric

Wadding (optional)

Ordinary sewing thread

Tapestry wool or 8-ply knitting wool, Blue

Assorted other woollen thread

Chenille needle

7 m (7 ¾ yd) of black satin bias binding

Several packets of small safety pins

CRAZY PATCHWORK

1 From the base cloth fabric, cut twelve 31 cm (12 ½ in) squares. Using the five-centre patch method or a combination of methods, crazy patch the twelve blocks. On each block, machine a row of zigzag stitches along the cutting line, trim any excess fabric. Hand-sew a row of basting on the stitching line.

2 Using woollen threads, cover all the seam lines with your choice of embroidery stitches. Embellish these rows of stitches with stitch combinations.

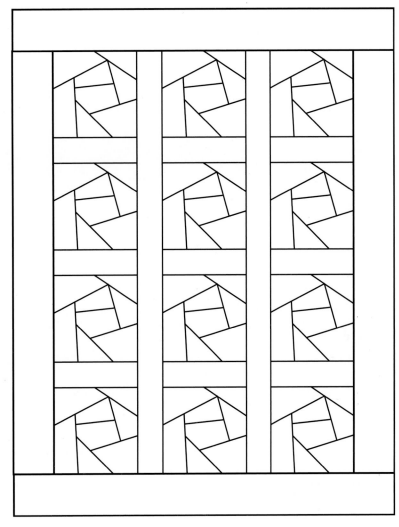

MAKING UP

1 From the calico, cut the backing fabric to measure 140 cm x 180 cm (56 in x 72 in). Place a clean sheet on the floor. Lay the backing fabric on the sheet and position the crazy squares on it, following the placement diagram.

2 From the red velvet, cut the following pieces:

- nine strips, each 8 cm x 31 cm (3 in x 12 ½ in);
- two strips, each 8 cm x 150 cm (3 in x 60 in);
- two strips, each 15 cm x 105 cm (6 in x 42 in); and
- two strips, each 15 cm x 180 cm (6 in x 72 in).

For the longer strips, you will have to join lengths.

3 Following the placement diagram below, stitch the blocks and the nine small strips into three long rows. Join the rows with a 150 cm (60 in) strip in between each pair.

4 Add the top borders, then the two side borders to the quilt top.

5 Lay the completed quilt top right side up on the calico backing, inserting a wadding layer, if desired. Make sure it is smooth and completely

wrinkle-free. Beginning in the middle, pin the layers together, using the safety pins.

6 Using the blue tapestry wool, feather stitch around each block. This does the double duty of holding the quilt layers together and decorating the seam lines at the same time.

7 Stitch, by hand or machine, a row of stitches close to the edge of the quilt top to hold the edges together. Trim any excess backing fabric. Unfold the satin bias binding and, using the fold line as a stitching guide, stitch the binding to the front of the quilt with the right sides together. Slipstitch the other side of the bias binding neatly to the back of the quilt.

Candlewicking Quilt

Classic cream, this superb quilt is sure to become a treasured heirloom.

MATERIALS

6 m (6 ⅔ yd) of 115 cm (45 in) wide homespun seeded fabric for the blocks and ruching

Sufficient fabric for the borders and backing (see the note below)

Sufficient thin wadding (see the note below)

Sufficient satin blanket binding

20 m (22 yd) of edging braid

Chenille needles, assorted sizes

Crewel needles, assorted sizes

Beeswax

Blue water-soluble marker pen

30 cm (12 in) embroidery hoop

DMC Stranded Cotton, Ecru

DMC Broder Cotton No. 16, Ecru

DMC Perle Cotton Nos 3, 5, 8, 12, Ecru

Crown Perle Rayon, Ecru

DMC Flower Thread, Ecru

Ordinary sewing cotton

Tracing paper

Black fineline permanent marker pen

Masking tape

Cotton tape

1 a	4 a	2 a
3	6	5 a
4 b	2 b	1 b
5 b	3	6

Note: The amount of fabric given here makes the twelve blocks with the ruching between. You will need to measure your bed and add borders appropriate to that particular bed and allow enough fabric for the backing, and enough wadding.

PREPARATION

See the embroidery designs on pages 188–193.

1 Preshrink all the fabric by washing it in hot water. Press the fabric while it is slightly damp.

2 Cut twelve 40 cm (16 in) squares from the homespun or 39.5 cm (15 ⅞ in) if you are using a precut quilter's block. From the remaining fabric, cut three strips 280 cm (112 in) long and 10 cm (4 in) wide. Cut eight strips 80 cm (32 in) long and 10 cm (4 in) wide.

3 To transfer the embroidery designs, trace each design from the pattern sheet, using the black marker pen. Tape the tracing to a window. Centre the fabric square over the tracing and trace the design onto the fabric, using the blue marker pen. There are six designs, all repeated once and stitched in

different cottons to give each one a slightly different look.

EMBROIDERY

Bind the hoop with the tape to prevent it leaving marks on the fabric, then place each square in turn in the hoop, work the embroidery in the stitches and threads indicated on the design, using the appropriate needles for the thread being used. Do not be concerned if the knots are flattened as you move the fabric around in the hoop. They will return after washing.

1 For block 1a, using a chenille needle and six strands of DMC Stranded Cotton that has been run through beeswax, stitch the four centre leaves in fishbone stitch. Using one strand of Perle 8 Cotton, stem stitch around the lead. Using Broder Cotton, couch the marked grid. With Perle 5 Cotton, stitch the border in herringbone stitch.

2 For block 1b, work in the same way as for 1a, except that the stem stitch outline is worked in Perle 5 Cotton, the couching is worked in the DMC Flower Thread and the herringbone is worked in Perle 3 Cotton.

3 For block 2a, stitch all the dots in colonial knots, using Perle 5 Cotton. Couch the grid on the hearts with the Crown Perle Rayon, stem stitching around the hearts in the same thread.

4 For block 2b, work in the same way as for 2a, except that the colonial knots are stitched in six strands of the stranded cotton and the hearts are

couched and outlined in the Broder Cotton.

5 For block 3, stitch the outline of the hearts in colonial knots using Perle 3 Cotton. Stitch the grid boxes using the Perle 12 Cotton, stitching the lines as marked and making sure you catch all the stitches with a catching thread. The dots in the centre box are colonial knots, stitched in two strands of Perle 12 Cotton. The squares are stitched in back stitch in one strand of Perle 12 Cotton.

6 For block 4a, stitch the dots in colonial knots, using Perle 3 Cotton. Using the Crown Perle Rayon, stitch the pattern in the leaf in running stitch; do not stitch the centre line. Stitch the outline of the leaf in stem stitch. Stitch the scroll designs in stem stitch in the Broder Cotton.

7 For block 4b, stitch the dots in colonial knots using the Perle 3 Cotton. Stitch the lines inside the leaf and the centre line in running stitch, using the Crown Perle Rayon. Stem stitch the outside of the leaf in Crown Perle Rayon. Work all the rest of the stitching in running stitch, using the Crown Perle Rayon.

8 For block 5a, stitch all the dots in colonial knots, using three strands of Broder Cotton. Do not stitch the tulips in the centre.

9 For block 5b, stitch all the dots in colonial knots, using six strands of stranded cotton. Stitch the tulip design in the centre, using six strands of stranded cotton and fishbone stitch. Stitch every second tulip

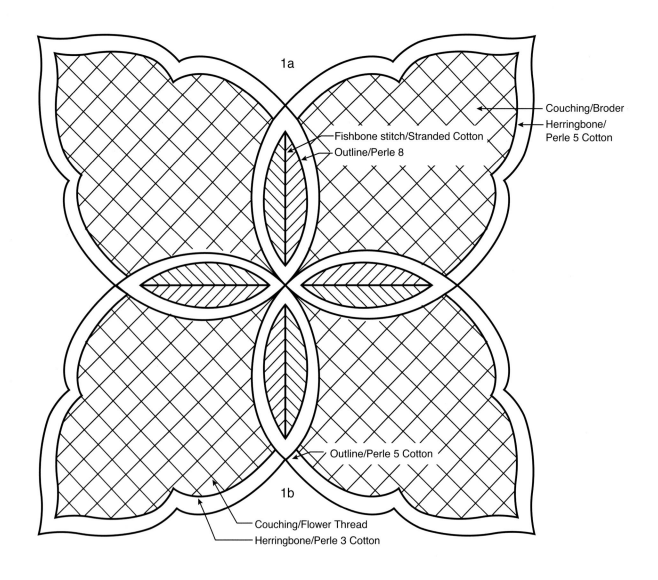

1a

Couching/Broder

Herringbone/
Perle 5 Cotton

Fishbone stitch/Stranded Cotton

Outline/Perle 8

Outline/Perle 5 Cotton

1b

Couching/Flower Thread

Herringbone/Perle 3 Cotton

centre in fly stitch instead of fishbone stitch, still using the stranded cotton.

10 For block 6, stitch all the dots in colonial knots, using Perle 3 Cotton. Stitch the rest of the design in running stitch, using the Crown Perle Rayon.

MAKING UP

1 Cut sixteen 40 cm (16 in) lengths of the braid. Stitch the braid to the right side of each block 6 mm (¼ in) from the side edges, with the finished side facing the design. Repeat this for all the blocks.

2 On the 80 cm (32 in) strips of homespun, sew two rows of gathering thread down each side, using the ordinary sewing thread. Gather up each strip to fit one side of the blocks. With the right sides facing, pin a gathered strip to one side of a block. Turn the block over so

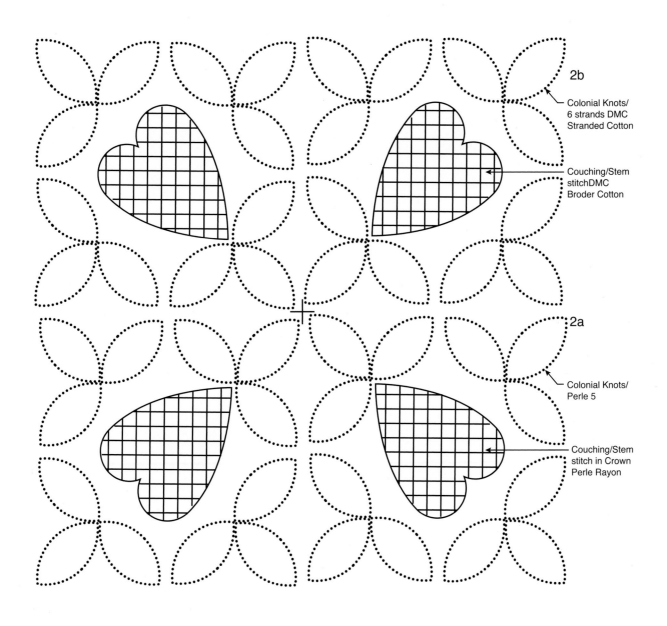

2b

Colonial Knots/
6 strands DMC
Stranded Cotton

Couching/Stem
stitchDMC
Broder Cotton

2a

Colonial Knots/
Perle 5

Couching/Stem
stitch in Crown
Perle Rayon

the back of the design faces you, and stitch the strip and the block together along the stitching line of the braid. Turn to the right side. Repeat this procedure until you have joined three blocks together with the ruched sashing in between. Make four rows of blocks and sashing.

3 Gather the long strips of homespun and attach the braid in the same way as before. Join the four rows to form the centre of the quilt. Cut and stitch braid around all the edges of the pieced centre.

4 Cut strips of homespun of the desired widths for the borders. Attach the borders to the four sides of the quilt.

5 Measure the quilt with the borders attached and cut the backing 10 cm (4 in) larger all around. Place the backing face down on a large table or the

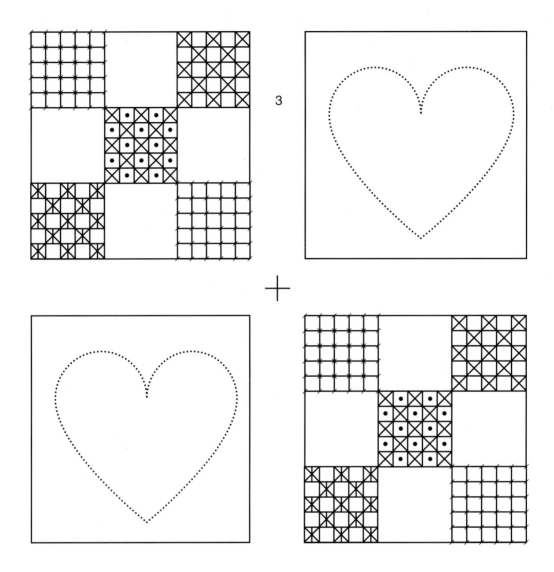

3

floor. Centre the wadding on top and then the quilt top on top of that. Baste the three layers together until the quilt is very firm, then quilt as desired. The pictured quilt has been stipple-quilted around the blocks and large borders with a small heart design for the

outside of the blocks. The quilting was done with a quilting machine. You can quilt with any design you choose.

6 When the quilting is completed, bind all the quilt edges with the blanket binding.

Cushions

To make any of these quilt blocks into cushions, cut and stitch the designs as instructed. Attach braid around the edges of the block as for the quilt. Cut a strip of fabric 20 cm x 230 cm (8 in x 92 in). Join the ends to form a loop. Press the

Colonial Knots/Perle 3
Running Stitch/Crown Perle Rayon
Stem stitch/Crown Perle Rayon

4a

4b

Colonial Knots/Perle 3
Running Stitch/Crown Perle Rayon
Stem stitch/Crown Perle Rayon

loop over double with the wrong sides facing. Sew two rows of gathering stitches 1.5 cm (⅝ in) from the raw edge and gather it up to fit the block. Pin the ruffle around the block, adjusting the gathering to make it even and placing a little extra fullness at the corners. Stitch the ruffle in place. Cut a 40 cm (16 in) square of fabric for the back. Sew the front to the back with the right sides facing, leaving an opening on one side, trim the seams and turn the cover right side out. You can either slipstitch the opening closed or insert a zipper.

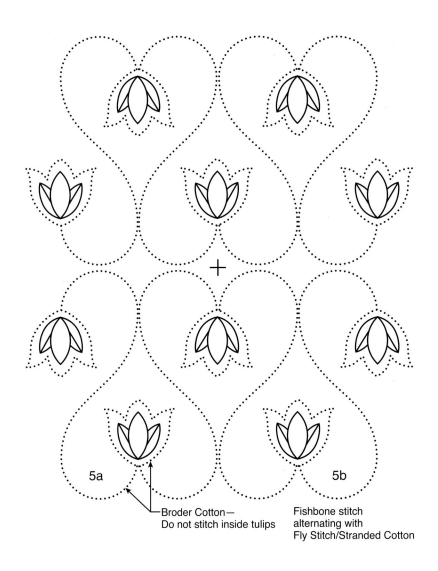

5a

5b

Broder Cotton—
Do not stitch inside tulips

Fishbone stitch
alternating with
Fly Stitch/Stranded Cotton

6

Colonial Knots/Perle 3
Running Stitch/Crown Perle Rayon

Magic Quilt

This magic quilt folds up and tucks into a sewn-on pocket, making a pillow! Every sofa needs pillows and something warm to snuggle into — how convenient to unwrap the pillow and find a cuddly quilt inside!

FABRIC SUGGESTIONS

We have chosen pre-printed cushion panels, with one extra panel for the sewn-on pocket into which the quilt folds away. For a different look, make the quilt from an all-over print, plain fabric, or piece one from a number of different fabrics. Remember that the pocket on the back of the quilt needs to have at least one side in the same fabric as the quilt back.

Left: The magic quilt opened out.
Above: Hand-quilt around the motifs for a different look.

Use a coordinating print to frame the pillow piece before sewing. The magic quilt folds into the pillow.
To fold the quilt: Place the quilt with the pocket facing downwards and fold in both side to cross over in the middle. Beginning at the end with no pocket, fold the quilt in pocket-sized lengths up to the pocket. Bring the pocket from the back to the front, turning it to contain the quilt as you go.

FINISHED SIZE

Quilt: 118 cm x 162 cm (47 in x 64 ¾ in)

Pocket: 45 cm x 45 cm (18 in x 18 in)

FABRIC QUANTITIES

170 cm (68 in) of 120 cm (48 in) wide fabric for the quilt top

170 cm (68 in) of 120 cm (48 in) wide fabric for the quilt back

46 cm x 50 cm (18 in x 20 in) for each side of the pocket

170 cm x 130 cm (68 in x 52 in) quilter's batting for the quilt

45 cm x 45 cm (18 in x 18 in) quilter's batting for the pillow

NOTIONS

Sewing thread

Safety pins, pine

Sewing machine

Cutting: 1 cm (⅜ in) allowances are included in the cutting instructions.

Cut out one quilt front, one quilt back and two pocket pieces in the sizes given.

CONSTRUCTION

1 With the right side facing upwards, place the quilt front over the batting. Pin-baste to secure.

2 With the right side facing upwards, place the pocket front over the batting. Pin-baste to secure. Place the pocket back over the front, with right sides together. Stitch around all the edges in a 1 cm (⅜ in) seam, leaving an opening for turning.

3 Turn the pocket to the right side and handsew the opening closed. Press. Machine-quilt through all thicknesses, following any lines on the front you wish to emphasise.

4 Place the pocket on the back of the quilt in the centre of one short end, 1 cm (⅜ in) in from the end. Stitch the pillow in place around three sides, with the opening facing the middle of the quilt. If you have used two coordinating fabrics, make sure the fabric that matches the back is facing upwards when you are positioning the pocket.

5 Place the quilt back over the quilt front, with right sides facing. Stitch around all the edges, leaving an opening for turning.

6 Turn the quilt to the right side and press. Handsew the opening closed. Tie the quilt through all the layers, where the 'blocks' intersect.

Postcards from the Past

This quilt is reminiscent of the quilts which were made in the middle of the 19th century, using a 'conversation' fabric. This is a fabric, often with a large print, which has many points of interest and can be successfully used in large areas. In this quilt, the conversation fabric has been used in the bands which separate the nine-patch blocks.

The quilt has been machine-pieced and hand-quilted.

Finished size: 150 cm x 165 cm (60 in x 67 in)

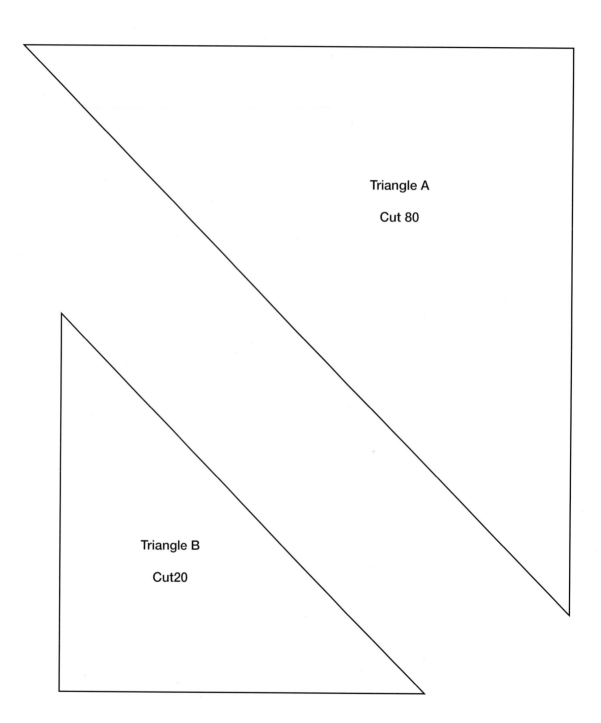

Triangle A

Cut 80

Triangle B

Cut20

MATERIALS

50 cm (20 in) of each of two floral fabrics

50 cm (20 in) of each of two plain fabrics

1 m (40 in) of print fabric for the triangles

2 m (80 in) of conversation fabric

50 cm (20 in) of fabric for the binding

3.4 m (3 yd 28 in) of backing fabric

155 cm x 170 cm (62 in x 68 in) of cotton wadding

Matching sewing thread

Scissors, or Olfa cutter and self-healing mat

Transparent ruler

Tracing paper

Sharp pencil

Quilting thread

Quilting needles (size 8 for beginners, size 10 for the more experienced)

METHOD

See the template on page 198.

6 mm (¼ in) seam allowances are included in all the measurements.

1 Cut the floral and the plain fabrics into 5 cm (2 in) strips, cutting across the full width of the fabric. Join three strips of

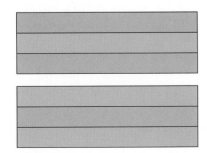

Fig 1

each floral/plain fabric combination into the strip sets shown in Fig. 1, making two of set 1 and one of set 2 for each fabric combination.

2 Cut the selvages of both ends of each strip set, then cut them into 5 cm (2 in) sections (Fig. 2).

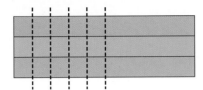

Fig 2

3 To form the blocks, join the sections made in step 2 as shown in Fig. 3, taking care to match the seams. Make 23 blocks of one fabric combination and 22 blocks of the other one. Press the blocks carefully.

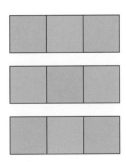

Fig 3

4 Trace and cut out the triangle templates from the pattern. Using Template A, cut out eighty triangles. Using Template B, cut out twenty triangles. Join an A triangle and a B triangle to opposite

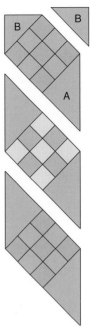

Fig 4

sides of each nine-patch block (Fig. 4). Press carefully.

5 Join nine of the nine-patch block and triangle combinations together into vertical rows, alternating the floral fabrics. Make three rows beginning with one fabric combination and two rows beginning with the other one. Join a B triangle at the ends of the rows to square them up. Press the rows carefully, taking care not to stretch the outer edges of the triangles which are on the bias.

6 Measure the length of the rows, measuring through the centre. Cut 14 cm (5 ½ in) wide side borders to this length. Join the pieced rows, alternating with the bands of the conversation fabric. Take care to alternate the two types of pieced rows as well.

FOR THE BORDERS

Measure the length of the quilt top, measuring though the centre. Cut 14 cm (5 ½ in) wide top and bottom borders to this length. Sew on the top and bottom borders. Press the quilt top well.

QUILTING

1 Cut the backing fabric in half lengthwise. Cut off the selvages on the inner edges, then rejoin the two halves to achieve a backing of the desired width.

2 Place the backing face down with the wadding on top and the quilt top on top of that, face upwards. Baste all the layers of the quilt sandwich together, beginning at the centre and working out to the edges. Baste around the outside edges (Fig. 5).

3 In keeping with the traditional look of this quilt, it has been hand-quilted quite closely in the patterns indicated (Fig. 6).

4 When the quilting is completed, trim the wadding and the backing to the size of the quilt top.

BINDING

1 Cut eight 6.5 cm (2 ½ in) wide strips across the full width of the fabric. You will need to join two strips together to reach the length required for each side of the quilt.

2 Press the binding over double with the wrong sides together and the raw edges even. On the right side of the quilt, sew the binding to the edges of the quilt (sides first, then the top and bottom) with the raw edges even. Turn the binding to the back of the quilt and slipstitch it in place, neatening the corners.

Don't forget to sign and date your quilt on the back.

Quilted Cushions

These pieced and quilted cushions have been designed as a pair and the only difference between them is in the varying ways the colours and prints have been used. As the lines are all straight, the design is also a pleasing way to show stripes and plaid fabrics.

FABRIC SUGGESTIONS

These cushions effectively combine plain and printed cotton fabrics of the same weight. They were selected from a coordinating range produced especially for patchwork.

FINISHED SIZE

40 cm (16 in) square, plus piping.

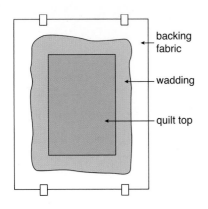

Fig 5

backing fabric

wadding

quilt top

Fig 6

FABRIC QUANTITIES

For each cushion:

20 cm (8 in) of 115 cm (45 in) wide fabric for the centre square and smaller corner squares

46 cm (18 ¼ in) square for back

Fabric for bias piping

Scrap pieces for side strips

NOTIONS

For each cushion:

Cushion insert

1.7 m (68 in) of piping cord

80 cm (32 in) fine quilter's batting

30 cm (12 in) zipper

CUTTING

Do not forget to add 1 cm (⅜ in) seam allowances to all the pieces you cut, except for the back panel which has 1 cm (⅜ in) seam allowances included.

FOR EACH CUSHION:

1 Cut one 20 cm (8 in) square for the centre, four 8 cm (3 in) squares for the corners, four strips 2 cm x 24 cm (¾ in x 9 ½ in) for the inner strips A, four strips 2 cm x 24 cm (¾ in x 9 ½ in) for the inner strips B, four strips 6 cm x 24 cm (2 ⅜ in x 9 ½ in) for the outer strips C, two panels 23 cm x 42 cm (9 in x 16 ¾ in) for the cushion back.

2 Cut sufficient 5 cm (2 in) wide bias strips to make 1.7 m (68 in) of bias piping.

CONSTRUCTION

3 Stitch two inner strips A to either side of the centre square, trimming off any excess level with the square.

4 Stitch two remaining strips A to the top and bottom of the centre square, stitching over the ends of the first A strips.

5 Stitch the inner strips B to the outer strips C along one long side. Stitch the B side of one of these pairs to an A strip on one side of the centre square. Stitch another one to the opposite A strip.

6 Stitch an 8 cm (3 in) square to each end of each remaining joined pair of strips. Centre and stitch each B edge to a remaining A edge, stitching across the ends of the previously sewn-on pairs of strips. Press well.

QUILTING

7 Fold the cushion front diagonally both ways and press a cross into the centre panel of the cushion.

8 Pin-baste the cushion top to the fine batting. Align the edge of the presser foot or your machine's quilting guide with the creases and stitch a triangle in each quarter of the centre panel. Continue making smaller triangles, using the presser foot or the quilting guide as your guide until the space is filled. Using the same technique, stitch squares in the corner squares.

FINISHING

9 Fold the piping strip in half, with wrong sides facing, enclosing the piping cord. Using the zipper foot of your sewing machine, stitch along close to the cord.

10 Baste the piping to the right side of the cushion front, with raw edges matching and the cord 1 cm (⅜ in) from the outer edge. Clip cord seam allowance at the corners for ease.

11 Place the two cushion backs together, right sides facing and raw edges matching. Stitch across one 42 cm (16 ¾ in) side taking a 2 cm (¾ in) seam allowance, and leaving a 30 cm (12 in) gap in the centre for the zipper. Press the seam open. Stitch the zipper into the opening. Open zipper.

12 Place the cushion front and back together, right sides facing. Stitch around the edge of the cushion, following the stitching line for the piping. Clip away excess fabric at corners. Turn the cushion to the right side, place the cushion insert inside and close the zipper.

Tied Patches

This quilt was made by piecing rectangles of brightly coloured cotton and then hand-tying them in the traditional way. You can make this bright and cheerful quilt in a weekend. Quilt it by sewing in the ditches of the seams between the patches or hand-quilting a design over the whole quilt top.

FINISHED SIZE

Quilt: 40 cm x 200 cm approximately (16 in x 80 in)

Block size: 30 cm x 30 cm (12 in x 12 in)

FABRIC QUANTITIES

36 rectangles of cotton fabric, in as many colours as possible

150 cm x 210 cm (approx.) (60 in x 84 in) backing fabric, pieced from 3 m (3 ¼ yd) of 115 cm (45 in) wide fabric

150 cm (60 in) black fabric for the borders and binding

150 cm x 210 cm (approx.) (60 in x 84 in) batting

NOTIONS

Thick crochet cotton for tying

Safety pins, pins, needles and scissors

Rotary (Olfa) cutter and mat

Plastic ruler and pencil

Sewing thread

Sewing machine

CUTTING

Do not forget to add seam allowances to each piece you cut.

1 Cut all the rectangles to 30 cm x 20 cm (12 in x 8 in) plus seam allowances. A rotary cutter will save time.

CONSTRUCTION

2 Lay out your quilt top (with six rectangles across and six down) and experiment with the arrangement. Join the top row together and then the next row. Continue in this way until you have six rows. Press. Mark them 1, 2, 3, 4, 5 and 6.

3 Join the six rows to complete the quilt top, following the order you have marked. Press.

4 Measure the width of the quilt top, measuring through the centre. Cut two strips of black fabric, each 9 cm (3 ½ in) plus seam allowances wide and as long as this measurement. Sew these to the top and bottom of the quilt top. Measure the length through the centre including the top and bottom borders. Cut two strips of black fabric 9 cm (3 ½ in) wide plus seam allowances and as long as this measurement. Sew these to the sides of the quilt. Press the quilt top carefully.

5 Lay the backing fabric on a table face down, and place the batting on top. Place the quilt top on top of that, face upwards. Baste or pin-baste through all thicknesses.

TYING

6 Using heavy crochet cotton, take a stitch at each corner and the centre of the rectangles. Tie the ends together twice securely, but don't pull too tightly. Trim the ends. For a more dramatic effect, use several strands of thread. Tie each one at these points. Trim off any excess backing and batting.

FINISHING

7 Measure the width of the quilt as before, to find the length of binding required. Cut two strips of black fabric, each 8 cm (3 in) wide and as long as this measurement. Press the strips over double with wrong sides together. Sew the binding to the top and bottom of the quilt with right sides facing and raw edges even. Turn the binding to the wrong side and handsew into place. Repeat this process for binding the side edges.

Stitch Guide

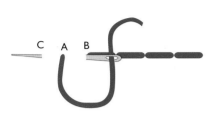

Back stitch

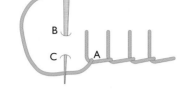

Blanket stitch

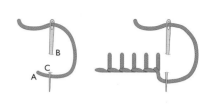

Buttonhole stitch

  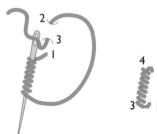

Bullion stitch

Chevron stitch

Colonial knot

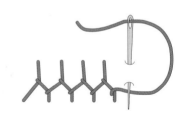

Cretan stitch

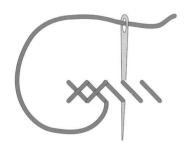

Cross stitch

Detached chain stitch

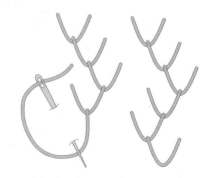

Double feather stitch

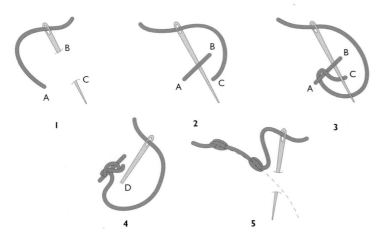

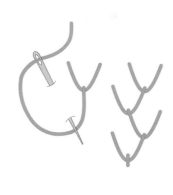

Double knot stitch

Feather stitch

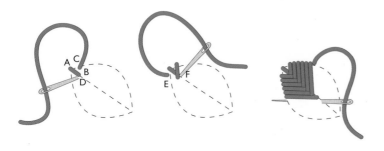

Fishbone stitch

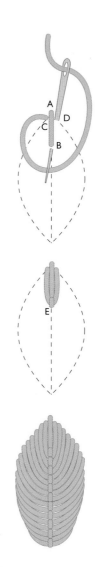

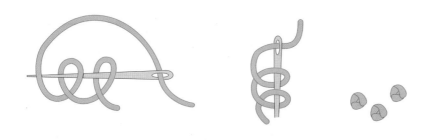

French knot

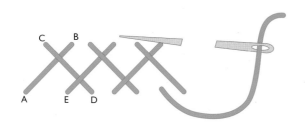

Herringbone stitch

Fly stitch

Lazy daisy stitch

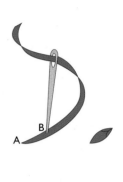

Ribbon stitch

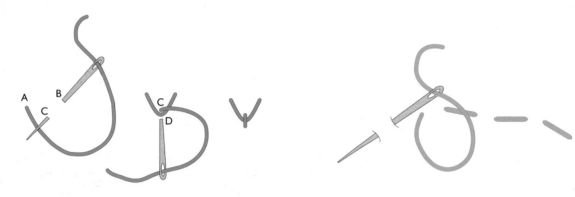

Open fly stitch

Running stitch

Stem stitch

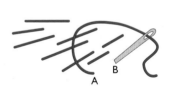

Straight stitch

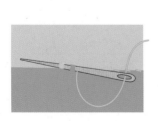

Slipstitch

Satin stitch

Straight stitch with small beads